Among the Rugged Peaks...

An Intimate Biography of Carla Laemmle

Original caricature of Carla Laemmle as she appeared in the 1931 Bela Lugosi version of *Dracula*. Copyright 2003, Illustration by Marshall Jay Kaplan.

Among the Rugged Peaks…

An Intimate Biography of Carla Laemmle

by Rick Atkins

Midnight Marquee Press, Inc.
Baltimore, Maryland

Copyright © 2009 by Rick Atkins
Interior layout and cover design by Susan Svehla
Copy Editing by Tom Proveaux

Without limiting the rights under copyright reserved above, no part of this publication may be reproduced, stored in or introduced into a retrieval system, or transmitted, in any form, or by any means (electronic, mechanical, photocopying, recording or otherwise), without the prior written permission of the copyright owner or the publishers of the book.

ISBN 13: 978-1-887664-91-2
ISBN 10: 1-887664-91-2
Library of Congress Catalog Card Number 2009920570
Manufactured in the United States of America

First Printing by Midnight Marquee Press, Inc., February 2009

Dedications

In Loving Memory of Ray Cannon
(1892-1977)

And

Carrie "Belle" Norton Laemmle
(1871-1962)

This book is dedicated to the beloved Bayer family
of Laupheim, Baden, Württemberg, Germany;
Udo, Gabi, Isabel and Mirko...

TABLE OF CONTENTS

Acknowledgments 9
Prologue 10

Act One
CHICAGO AND THE WESTWARD MOVE
(1909-1921)

Scene One
Little Miss Rebekah and Her Land of Dreams 19

Scene Two
Beth's Universal Experience/1921–1934 34

Act Two
CARLA' S RAY OF LIGHT

Her Majesty the Prince/1935 -1977 80

Act Three
MOVING FORWARD IN LIFE 145

Epilogue 191
Notes 194
Selected Bibliography 201
Appendix 203
Carla Laemmle Photo Archive 205
Index 216

When Earth's Last Picture is Painted
Rudyard Kipling (1892)

When Earth's last picture is painted
and the tubes are twisted and dried,

When the oldest colours have faded,
and the youngest critic has died,

We shall rest, and, faith, we shall need it —
lie down for an aeon or two,

Till the Master of All Good Workmen
shall put us to work anew.

And those that were good shall be happy:
they shall sit in a golden chair;

They shall splash at a 10-league canvas
with brushes of comets' hair;

They shall find real saints to draw from—
Magdalene, Peter, and Paul;

They shall work for an age at a sitting
and never be tired at all!

And only the Master shall praise us,
and only the Master shall blame;

And no one shall work for money,
 and no one shall work for fame,

But each for the joy of the working, and each, in his separate star,
Shall draw the Thing as he sees It
for the God of Things as They are!"

—Ray and Carla's favorite poem

Acknowledgments

The author would like to thank the following people who shared their time during the research for this book. They are listed as follows: David Simeur, Arnold Stern, JoAnn Surber, Kathleen Simeur Searl, Forrest J Ackerman, Michal Kerestes, Angelo Gavrilos, Zachary Zito, Stephen Gallagher, Anji Holtzman, Jeff Pirtle, Sandra R. Williamson, Susan Fleishmann, Marshall Jay Kaplan, former German Mayor, Otmar Schick and to the Citizens of Laupheim, Baden Württemberg, Germany; you know who you are. Special thanks to Scott and Elizabeth MacQueen for years of hospitality and warmth, my brother Dean, my sisters, Martha and Kathy for their love and support. Also to the ever present talents of Gary J. Svehla and his lovely wife, Susan Svehla . Meeting up again has been a joy for all! Posthumous thanks go to my dear mother, Faye Atkins who remains the strongest inspiration in my life, with love always. Also to the memory of Ruth and Eddie Regis, Carole Laemmle Bergerman, Ruthe Kanakoff, and to Stanley and Fay Bergerman, and Evelyn Moriarty and Forrest J Ackerman for their loyal friendship. And last but not least, to Josephine Simeur, and Ray Cannon whose enduring spiritual presence continues to humble me. Special thanks are extended to the following organizations;, The Newberry Library of Chicago; The Chicago Public Library; The University of Illinois at Champaign/Urbana Alumni Association; The Urbana Free Library; Mount Hope Cemetery & Mausoleum of Champaign, Illinois; Rosehill Cemetery of Chicago; The UCLA Archives, The Natural History Museum of Los Angeles County, and Universal Studios (at Universal City, California). And finally to Carla, who has made this all possible. You are amazing! I love you! I will never forget our days in Germany together nor the "Monk fish!" May God bless each and every one of you.

Prologue

Some movie fans may ask, who *is* Carla Laemmle? Let's begin at the beginning. Nearly 100 years ago she was born Rebekah Isabelle Laemmle, the only daughter of Joseph and Carrie "Belle" Norton Laemmle, who were residents of Chicago, Illinois. It is this period of American history that sets her story apart from other film bios, for Rebekah Isabelle, or Carla as she became known, is the niece of the late movie mogul, Carl Laemmle, founder of Universal Pictures Corporation.

Carl Laemmle and his older brother, Joseph, were German immigrants who had successfully made "good" in America. However, as Joseph advanced in years, his brother, Carl, asked that he and his family relocate to California.

In January 1921, at the age of 11, young Carla with her parents and maternal grandmother, Emogene Isabelle Norton, made the big move from Chicago to Universal City, California, a fledgling six-year-old incorporated community on 230 acres of land in Lankershim Township, which is on the north side of the Hollywood Hills. Mr. Laemmle purchased it for $165.000.00. Universal City was dedicated solely to the making of motion pictures.

Carla had studied dance since the age of six and won notoriety in Chicago as a prodigious success. Upon arrival in California, she was enrolled in the Ernest Belcher School of Dance. At the age of 16, then known as Beth Laemmle, she was cast in a small part as the Prima Ballerina in the 1925 Universal production, *The Phantom of the Opera* starring Lon Chaney, "the man of a thousand faces." Her greatest claim to fame was summed up this way:

> Uncle Carl's poor brother Joe's little girl, "Rebekah," "Beth," "Carla," has become the last surviving member of that illustrious branch of the Laemmle family and the mantle of celebrity has thereby fallen upon me!

Growing up at Universal was a life-changing experience for Miss Laemmle. She witnessed the filming of several of her uncle's classic movie productions, many of which took place on the backlot. A small part in a 1931 Universal movie would earn Carla Laemmle a cult following. The movie was *Dracula,* which starred Bela Lugosi. Carla appears as one of the passengers in the opening scene, whose coach travels through the Carpathian Mountains. Carla's one line is now a classic bit of fanboy trivia, "Among the rugged peaks that frown down upon the Borgo Pass, are found crumbling castles of a bygone age."

Carla remained with Universal Pictures until the studio was sold in 1936. Carla and her family moved from Universal in April 1937. She credits her Uncle Carl Laemmle for much in her life and shares her memories of him between these covers. Until 1949 Carla worked as a dancer in films for a variety of studios.

Carla on her 87th birthday with the author, October 20, 1996.

I have had the privilege of becoming Carla Laemmle's official biographer since befriending her on her 87th birthday. We first began a written correspondence, thanks to Stanley Bergerman (son-in-law to Mr. Carl Laemmle), who suggested that I write to Carla. In fact, it was Stanley and his charming wife, Fay Bergerman, who arranged for the first of what became "double birthday celebrations." Although I had an association with the Laemmle family for many years, I had never met Carla. Through correspondence we discovered our birthdays were one day apart, Carla's on October 20 and mine on October 21, although 49 years separates us.

The Sunday morning I met Miss Laemmle, I saw an extremely agile woman walking resolutely toward my car. Her years as a professional dancer had kept her spry and agile. As I opened the passenger door for Carla and she removed her sunglasses, I was quite taken by her beauty. She began directing the way to San Vincente Boulevard and before you know it, we had become so caught up in conversation that we realized we had missed our exit. In fact, we were lost several times over! Asking others for directions became routine before we ultimately found our destination.

The Bergermans were singing "Happy Birthday" to us when we finally made it into the banquet room at the Brentwood Country Club. We still laugh about that day. My very first autograph from Carla was inscribed with the following.

> October 20, 1996—my birthday—Dear Rick, Meeting you and enjoying this happy day with you was the most fun of all, especially getting lost! We must do it again. Love, Carla Laemmle.

Our written correspondence began mushrooming soon thereafter, week after week, month after month, and year after year. More visits and "double-birthday" celebrations continued to enhance our growing friendship. The most memorable time spent with Carla Laemmle was in the summer of 1999. We found ourselves boarding an airplane en route to Europe. Five months prior, Carla had invited me to be her guest in the Province of Baden Laupheim, Württemberg, Germany.

At the invitation of then-Mayor Otmar Schick, Carla and I spent nine unforgettable days in the homeland of the Laemmle family. We were houseguests of Dr. Udo Bayer, co-curator of the Laupheim Museum [SchloBGroBlaupheim Museum zur Geschichte von Christen & Juden]

Then Laupheim Mayor, Otmar Schick (right) with Carla and the author (Laupheim, Württemburg, Germany, July 24, 1999).

and his charming wife, Gabriele. It was Udo Bayer who suggested I write Carla's biography. In fact, Dr. Bayer encouraged me to write it. Having another manuscript in the works, I hesitated until it was completed. Finally, I phoned Carla and asked her if she would consider allowing me to write her story. Instead of an answer, Carla's question to me was, "Why me?—No one is going to know who I am?" Then I explained Udo Bayer had suggested the idea. Carla said with a chuckle, "Oh, I guess Udo thinks I am going to die soon! What do you *really* think about writing it Rick?" I answered, "Of course, I would love to write your story."

A good portion of material that she has stored for years consisted of family documentation, a wealth of written correspondence and her treasury of over 160 photographs, many of which are included in this book. As I write this, a four-inch tall Precious Moments ballerina figurine is a treasured gift from Carla to always remind me that she remains "on her toes." Carla once told me:

> If my life on earth were to be made into a Play, I feel that it should be done in Three Acts.

Therefore, in writing her story I composed it in three acts. Portions were transposed from family research compiled by Carla's mother, Belle Laemmle. Her in-depth study began at Chicago's Newberry Library as early as 1901. From this family history, it was learned that Carla Laemmle shares lineage with four past Presidents of the United States: Grover Cleveland, Ulysses S. Grant, Millard Fillmore and Gerald R. Ford.

Among Carla's blessings was an extraordinary 42-year relationship with motion picture writer, director and author, the late Raymond Cannon. Carla writes:

> He was a gifted, highly evolved human being...Ray was the love of my life...when I met Ray he changed the way I thought about myself...Ray instilled Magic in me! He wrote an enchanting Chinese play for me [*Her Majesty the Prince*] and we got it produced. From that time I was Princess Quan Mui Mai...I loved it!

Ray Cannon, Carla Laemmle and Carla's mother, Mrs. Joseph (Belle) Laemmle, were among a small group of Old China enthusiasts

1920s Columbia publicity still of actor, director and writer, Raymond Cannon.

who began meeting at the Golden Dragon Café in China City. Together, this group helped form (between 1938 and 1939) the Chinese Culture Society in Los Angeles.

We have set the stage by including in the prologue circumstances and history surrounding the lives of Joseph Laemmle and Belle Norton and their families prior to their wedding. Belle Norton was originally from Connecticut, the small town of Colebrook River, to be exact. Colebrook River is located in northwest Connecticut on the Massachusetts border. Belle was an only child. Her father, Edward Daniel Norton, who had lost a leg in the Civil War, had been separated from his wife, Emogene Isabelle Loomis Norton (better known as "Emma"). Therefore, Belle was reared in Urbana from the age of 12 by her mother and maternal grandparents, Amelia (Long) and Oliver P. Loomis, who was a former Lieutenant in the Civil War. It was a predominantly Presbyterian household.

Belle spoke fluent German, which she used in composing her college thesis *On the Influence of the Accent on the Language, with Special Reference to the German Language*. During Belle's college years, she occasionally traveled to Chicago to visit relatives and study the family history. It was on one of Belle's visits that she met 54-year-old Joseph Laemmle. They met at a B'hai faith meeting in Chicago at the Masonic Temple in the summer of 1908.

It was on January 17, 1909 in Urbana, Illinois that Joseph Laemmle married Carrie Belle Norton. Belle was a 37-year-old bride, who had graduated Valedictorian from the University of Illinois at Urbana/Champaign, Class of 1907.

Joseph Laemmle was a German-born Jewish immigrant from the southern tip of the Bavarian Forest, a province known as Laupheim, Württemberg. He was the first-born of the 13 children born to Rebekkah and Julius Baruch Laemmle. Rebekkah Laemmle was a loving wife and mother, who was adored by all of her children. She enchanted young Joseph with the German language and by reading to him and faithfully took her children to the Synagogue in Laupheim. Julius Baruch (better known as J.B. Laemmle) was a self-taught businessman, a visionary and a stern father. His father's business demeanor in the face of adversity impressed Joseph.

School photo of Belle Norton at the age of 12. This was her first year living in Urbana, Illinois.

Eight of the 13 Laemmle children passed away before the age of seven. Aside from Joseph, the surviving siblings were Louis, Carl, Karoline and Siegfried. Much of Joseph's early life was encompassed by war, although none of the armed conflict directly involved the German commoners.

With the blessings of his parents, young Joseph Laemmle immigrated to America in late 1871. Joseph Laemmle's adventure to the new world began the same year Belle Norton was born. He arrived in New York City soon before his 18th birthday in January 1872. Life in New York, while a struggle for young Joseph, was also full of excitement and promise for the quintessential salesman quickly learned the English language and lived in New York until he relocated to Chicago in 1882. Three years later, a twist of fate changed Joseph's life. He became the manager of the subscription department of a popular German newspaper, the *Illinois Staatszeitung* at 171 Washington Street. Part of Joseph's daily routine was opening and reading the *Staatszeitung*'s mail. He came upon a letter from a man of 18 who had emigrated from Germany to New York and was searching the whereabouts of his eldest brother of whom he had lost touch. The letter was signed "Carl Laemmle"—Joseph's younger brother, who was a mere toddler when he had immigrated to America. In those days, keeping in touch with one's family wasn't as easy as it is nowadays. Joseph was overwhelmed and amazed to be in receipt of a letter from his own brother. He immediately contacted Carl and sent him $10 to come to Chicago, where he promised to help Carl find employment. This was not an easy task. For the next two years Carl would hold various jobs and eventually the dissatisfaction got the best of Carl. He talked his brother Joseph into returning for a visit to their native homeland.

Joseph's other surviving siblings were respectively, Louis, Carl, Karoline (Bernheim) and Siegfried Laemmle. (Laupheim, Germany, 1920.)

The trip home would be Joseph's first visit since immigrating to America 15 years earlier. Arriving in Laupheim they visited their 67-year-old father Julius Baruch Laemmle and paid tribute to their deceased mother Rebekkah who had passed away four years earlier.

Joseph and Carl brought another brother with them back to America, Louis and also Joseph's first bride, Paula Beidermann, with whom he had begun corresponding with through the *Illinois Staatszeitung.* The couple married in Stüttgart. From their union a son was born in Chicago on October 25, 1887 named Edward Laemmle. The marriage would last only eight years.

Joseph Laemmle later relocated to Muscatine, Iowa by himself. He was employed as a film equipment salesman for the fledgling nickelodeon business. Carl had relocated to Oshkosh, Wisconsin where he spent 12 years working for the Continental Clothing Company. There Carl married German-born Recha Stern. Louis Laemmle continued living on Chicago's south side, employed as a baker.

When Carl Laemmle returned to Chicago in 1906, he was in search of a storefront for a five and ten cent store. His ideas soon changed after Joseph took him to a downtown nickelodeon—Carl was amazed to see film in motion. Laemmle rented a storefront on Chicago's Milwaukee Avenue from an undertaker—it came with 120 folding chairs. With Joseph Laemmle's help Carl opened his theatre on February 26, 1906. It was christened The White Front (a.k.a. Laemmle's Five-Cent Movie Theatre). Needless to say, the business was a huge success. Joseph Laemmle then became manager of the Family Theatre in Muscatine. In addition he trav-

Once Carl Laemmle's White Front Theater, in Chicago, this is the facade as it looked in 1986 (photograph by the author).

1905 newspaper advertisement: "Take a vacation for your health." The Battle Creek Sanitarium is where Joseph Laemmle frequented between before his marriage to Belle Norton.

eled the roads of the Midwest opening, operating and selling nickelodeons. It was during a stop in Chicago that Joseph Laemmle met Belle Norton. Joseph's health was Belle's major concern at this time in his life. He would make several visits to Michigan's famed Battle Creek Sanitarium where he sought rest and would partake of nutritional eating and exercise regimes to ensure good health. A written correspondence ensued between Mr. Laemmle and Miss Norton while Joseph was still employed on the road. A large number of Joseph Laemmle's letters to Belle were written in German and were clearly love letters.

When Joseph asked for Belle's hand in marriage he wrote to Mrs. Emma Norton as well to ask for her approval. Emma pondered for several months over the wisdom of allowing her gentile daughter to marry a Jewish man, who was many years Belle's senior. Emma finally met Joseph Laemmle and graciously gave her blessings.

Among the Rugged Peaks…An Intimate Biography of Carla Laemmle is an interpretation of one life during our changing times with a real-life cast of characters.

Allow yourself to go back in time with the birth of a girl whose life was forever changed after a move from Chicago to Los Angeles. Carla herself writes some of the narratives throughout—about her impassioned life and the people in it. The aim is to accurately document history as well as to entertain the reader as Carla approaches her 100th birthday.

Act One
Chicago and the Westward Move
1909-1921

Scene One
Little Miss Rebekah and Her Land of Dreams

Soon after Joseph Laemmle's marriage to Belle Norton, the newlyweds relocated to Chicago, Illinois. Brother Louis Laemmle resided at Forest Avenue on Chicago's South side and helped the couple set up their new residence at 4231 South Calumet Avenue.

Nearly nine months to the day of their marriage, Belle gave birth to a daughter at Chicago's Michael Reese Hospital on Wednesday, October 20, 1909 at 9 a.m. The child was named Rebekah Isabelle Laemmle.[1]

Rebekah Isabelle Laemmle would use several names during her fascinating life. For the sake of simplicity and clarity, we will use the name she is known by today, Carla.

William Howard Taft was America's 27th President and the *Chicago Daily Tribune* cost two cents. The biggest news story of October 20, 1909 was the announced plans

Joseph Laemmle married Belle Norton January 17, 1909 in Urbana, Illinois.

Rebekah Isabelle Laemmle, November 1909, Chicago, Illinois.

for a Pennsylvania Railroad Depot that would make way for the building of a new $25,000.00 Chicago-Northwestern Train Terminal.

Joseph Laemmle notified Grandmother Emma of her granddaughter's birth via a postcard dated October 26, 1909 in which Joseph wrote:

> Dear Mama, The improvement of my dear wife is more marked from day to day, and she is resting as far as strength is concerned, she is the same as before her confinement. The Baby is splendid and is a real American Beauty in miniature. We all send our love to you. Yours as ever, Joseph.

After Carl made a moderate success in the nickelodeon business, he turned to film distribution. The Laemmle Film Service grew to include regional offices throughout the Midwest and New York.

In the winter of 1908, Carl sold his five-cent movie theatre on Chicago's Milwaukee Avenue as well as Carl's Family Theatre located on Halstead Street. The original location, known as the White Front Theatre, was taken over by the Peto brothers under Joseph Laemmle's supervision. The business operated under the name Peto-Laemmle Theatre until it was dissolved in 1910 and everyone went their separate way.

One of the major problems facing theater owners and film producers was the Edison Patents Company or "The Trust" as it was known, who had a monopoly on film production, cameras and film stock and a legal team that would take any rebel to court. Laemmle was a member of the Edison Patents Company at first, but refused to pay royalties to them for film production. In 1909 he withdrew and began to produce his own films using French Lumière film rather than Edison film stock. In 1910 he founded the Motion Picture Distributing and Sales Company in New York City and boldly declared himself an independent who would wage a long, tough battle in the courts against "The Trust." Laemmle fought more than 280 lawsuits from the Patents Company and rallied for the cause. The cases were eventually abolished by judicial decision in 1915.

Laemmle is credited with introducing the star system by launching Florence Lawrence as the first major movie star. He also introduced

The Carl Laemmle Family in 1910 - (left to right) Recha (Stern) Laemmle, Julius (later Carl Junior), Rose (later Rosabelle) Laemmle, Carl Laemmle.

Mary Pickford, who later became known as America's Sweetheart to filmgoers.

Carl Laemmle's first IMP production was a one-reel adaptation of Longfellow's poem *Hiawatha* starring Gladys Hulette. The confident exhibitor, now turned film producer, advertised, "You can bet it is classy, or it wouldn't be my first release!" Mr. Laemmle personally obtained exclusive European production rights, a practice that was not very common at that point in time. Laemmle began producing films at the Actophone studio, which was located on 11th Avenue and 53rd Street in New York. *Hiawatha* was shot in New Jersey using a Pathé camera. The 15-minute silent film opened October 25, 1909 in New York City, premiering five days after Carla's birth.

Carl Laemmle soon relocated to New York with his 35-year-old wife Recha Stern. Carl and Recha were married August 28, 1898 in Oshkosh, Wisconsin. Recha was the niece of Carl's employer, Sam Stern. The couple had two children, son Julius (later known as Carl Laemmle, Jr.), was born in Chicago in 1908, and daughter Rosabelle, who was born in Oshkosh, Wisconsin in 1901.

Joseph's brother Louis had married Frieda Heller in Ichenhausen, Germany in April 1911. Frieda was a cousin to a former business partner of brother Carl.

In April 1912 (soon after the luxury ship *Titanic* sank), Joseph Laemmle returned to real estate, which he would continue to sell until 1920. Joseph and his family relocated to an area of Chicago known as Washington Park in 1913.[2] For seven years they resided at 6132 South

Langley Street where Carla attended the Austin O. Parsons Elementary School until the age of 11.

"Granma" Emma Norton remained in Urbana although occasional visits did take place traveling via train. As a child, little Carla had a fondness for four-legged creatures that began with a variety of toys before acquiring live friends. She recalled having a pet turtle named JoJo that she took with her in a small box as the family rode the train to Granma's house. Before reaching their destination, Carla peered in on JoJo and discovered that the turtle had escaped. "My father had half the passengers on the train looking for a turtle that was never found."

By 1913 Carl's brother-in-law Maurice Fleckles, who had married Recha Stern's sister Anna in 1906, was managing the Laemmle Film Service headquarters in Chicago. Louis Laemmle was appointed assistant manager of the Laemmle Film Service while Carl traveled between New York to Southern California. Laemmle operated two small film production studios in California in addition to his IMP studio in New York. The locations were not adequate for film productions. Laemmle needed more space and a location where weather conditions would not affect filming.

Carl Laemmle opened the gates of Universal City on March 15, 1915. The new Universal City was a 230-acre ranch that was located in South-

Carl Laemmle proudly opens the gates to Universal City, March 15, 1915 having the gold key presented to him by opera diva, and Universal's star police chief, Laura Oakley.

President Woodrow Wilson meets Carl Laemmle and his fellow motion picture investors who helped establish Universal Pictures (1915).

ern California's San Fernando Valley. The land had been purchased by Isadore Bernstein, Laemmle's chief builder, for $165,000 in the name of Universal Pictures (a.k.a. The Universal Film Manufacturing Company). The new company was the result of a merger that was finalized Saturday, June 8, 1912 in New York City between Laemmle's IMP Company, Pat Power's, Powers Motion Picture Co., William Swanson's Rex Motion Picture Co., Mark Dintenfass' Champion Film Co., David Horsley's Nestor Film Co. and Charles Baumann and Adam Kessel's New York Motion Picture Company.

Carl Laemmle was the first of the studio moguls to build a community solely dedicated to the making of motion pictures. U.S. President Woodrow Wilson met with Laemmle and the investors of Universal City to congratulate them on this bold business venture. In its first year, Universal produced 250 movies under the supervision of "Uncle Carl," as he would become known.[3]

To help understand this period in time,1915, Woodrow Wilson was serving the third year of his first term as 28th President.[4] The first long distance telephone service between New York and San Francisco was demonstrated and the one-millionth Ford automobile rolled off an assembly line in Detroit, Michigan. Moviemaker, D.W. (David Wark) Griffith's

Civil War epic *The Birth of a Nation* opened to much controversy because of its depiction of the Ku Klux Klan.[5]

Meanwhile, back in the windy city, Chicago's Jazz Age was hopping on the city's south side, and in the nearby Italian district gangster activity was on the rise and over 50 bombs exploded within the first five months of 1915.

That same year the world was shocked by the sinking of the British steamship *Lusitania* on Friday, May 7. The ocean liner was sunk off the coast of Ireland by a German submarine—there were 1,924 persons aboard and 1,198 drowned, 114 of which were Americans. Indignation over the sinking led the United States into WWI.[6]

Back in Urbana, Emma Norton's niece Grace A. Campbell, Carla's second cousin, met Ralph Danielson, who was originally from New Jersey. He had been living in Urbana while Grace was a student at the University of Illinois. Ralph was well liked by Grace's mother Carrie Loomis and her sister, Emma Norton. As it turned out, Grace Campbell and Carla Laemmle were the last two female descendants of the Loomis/Norton families.

Grace Amelia Campbell graduated from the University of Illinois Urbana/Champaign, in Liberal Arts and Sciences in the summer of 1915. Soon after that Grace and Ralph took a Chicago train trip to meet Ralph's family which turned out to occur during a disastrous heat wave that claimed the lives of 535 people in Cook County.

Back in Washington Park Little Carla was six years old. Her mother once told her that from the way Carla had kept wiggling her little toes, she knew her daughter

Little Rebekah at age six in Professor Henri Jacobson's dance school, Chicago, Illinois

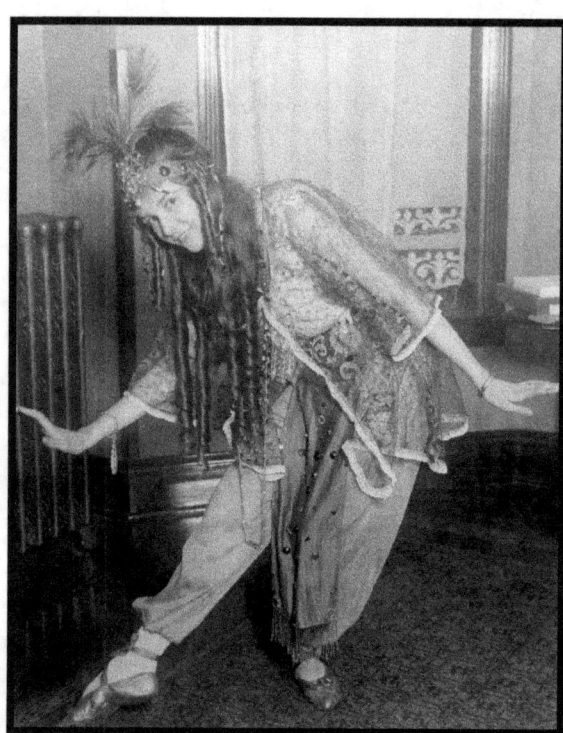
Rebekah's neighborhood friend, Mary Philbin (age 12) with her real life hair. (Chicago, 1915).

wanted to be a dancer. In fact, Carla continued to show so much talent for dancing her mother hired Professor Henri Jacobson, Maitre de ballet. Jacobson would give private lessons to Carla for four years. From the age of eight she also took three years of piano lessons with Dr. Balatka at the Chicago Musical College.

Carla also displayed a marked talent for poetry. Some of her writings were published in Chicago newspapers. The *Chicago Herald and Examiner* once wrote, "Rebekah [Carla] is only half as old as was the famous poet Milton when he commenced to 'make rhymes'," and "Six year old girl entertains with extemporaneous poetry."

Neighbor Mary Philbin (yes, the Lon Chaney's and *The Phantom of the Opera*'s Mary Philbin) and five-year-old Carla became fast friends. Mary and her parents, Blanche and John Philbin, lived on nearby 61st Street, and they were friends and neighbors for four years. Carla remembered her childhood friend with the following written words:

> As it just happened, my family and Mary Philbin's were neighbors in those very early years in Chicago... Although Mary was six years older than I, there was a certain innocence and childlike quality about her that seemed to equalize our ages thereby making the difference unimportant.
>
> In 1915, I was six years old and Mary was 12... What can I say about Mary Philbin that doesn't come off like

some Hollywood press agent hype? I simply adored and worshipped her beauty. To me, her exquisite beauty set her apart from other mortals. Her origin most surely was from Venus. Her cameo-like features were like finely chiseled alabaster. Her luxuriant, soft brown curls reached down below her waist, and there was a gentle sweetness and fragile delicacy about her. She was simply angelic, a living angel...

This was Mary Philbin to me. And yet I was never jealous of her. She was like a being from a world where only goodness and beauty reigned... As time went by and Mary matured she appeared to grow even more beautiful.

Friday March 24, 1916, Grace Campbell became Mrs. Ralph Danielson. The ceremony took place at the Humboldt Presbyterian Church. Joseph, Belle and Carla Laemmle, now age seven, attended the wedding and dinner held at the groom's family residence in Chicago, The bride's mother, Carrie Loomis Campbell, was also present.

During this period in time Woodrow Wilson was inaugurated to a second term as President. He campaigned on the slogan, "He kept us out of war!" However, that was not to be. Wilson appeared before Congress and outlined his conditions for American participation in the war. The United States declared war on Germany on Friday, April

Little Miss Rebekah Laemmle (Chicago, Illinois 1917)

In Hollywood, Universal was turning out numerous comedic shorts such as the 1915 *How Billy Got His Raise*.

6, 1917. President Wilson asked that the present conflict be resolved in such a way as to leave no aftermath of bitterness in the hearts of the defeated—a "Peace with Victory."

Back in Chicago, Grace Campbell Danielson later would give birth to James Campbell Danielson on March 17, 1917. Her son was named after Grace's late father, James A. Campbell. Unfortunately, James Campbell Danielson lived only four days.[7]

Today we take for granted a childhood safe from world wars and most fatal diseases. But our grandparents were not so lucky. In December 1909, the Nicaraguan Civil War nearly had the United States involved until a treaty enacted by executive agreement by President Taft was signed which ended that war by 1911. Six years later in early December 1917, the United States declared war on Austria-Hungary. Nearly one year later, a Monday in 1918, the 11th day of the 11th hour, of the 11th month, "the war to end all wars" ended (after conflict that began in 1914).[8] Although the world war was over, another war was on the horizon. Pandemonium hit the world during the year of 1918 when an influenza virus epidemic swept the world, killing between 20 and 40 million people.[9] Many children lost their entire families to the innocent sounding flu.

And strangely enough, when the world could have used a good stiff drink, the Congress in it's infinite wisdom ratified The 18th Amendment to the Constitution which prohibited the manufacture, import and export and the sale of alcoholic beverages anywhere in the United States of America. This was the beginning of Prohibition. And we all know how well that worked out.

During these times Mrs. Carl Laemmle, better known as Recha, enjoyed summers with her husband and children at their summer home in Edgemere on Long Island, New York. It was here that Recha befriended Mrs. Henrietta Thalberg, whose mother lived next door to the Laemmles. Henrietta had a 17-year-old son, who was above average intelligence and fascinated by moving pictures. Mr. Laemmle saw promise in the stridently independent young man—Irving Thalberg, and Laemmle hired the 19-year-old to be his personal secretary. Also hired with Thalberg was Dan Ross Lederman, a senior branch executive at the Universal offices on Broadway Avenue in Manhattan. Thalberg started out with a salary of $35 per week.[10]

Recha Laemmle passed away on Monday evening, January 12, 1919 at the Laemmle home at 378 West End Avenue in New York. She was just 43 and had been married for 21 years. Recha was survived by her husband Carl (age 51), her daughter Rosabelle (now 17) and her son Julius ("Junior," age 10), as well as her two sisters, Frieda and Mrs. Anna Fleckles and three brothers, Herman, Abe and Julius Stern. Recha's cause of death was listed as pneumonia, brought on by influenza. She was laid to rest at Salem Fields Cemetery in Brooklyn, New York. Carl Laemmle never remarried. Little Carla Laemmle would never know her Aunt Recha.[11]

During the year of 1919 Carla turned 10; her mother, Belle turned 48 (nine days after Valentines Day) when Grandmother, Emma Norton turned 74. Louis Laemmle continued to manage operations at the Chicago office of the Universal Film Manufacturing Company.

In addition, the year 1919 saw events occurring such as the dial telephone introduced by the American Telephone and Telegraph Company. The Radio Corporation of America (RCA) was established by the General Electric Company. Woodrow Wilson suffered a heart attack and a stroke from which he would never fully recover, however he completed his second term as President. Race riots erupted in 26 United States cities including Washington D.C. and Chicago. The Communist Party was formed in Chicago, which President Wilson made illegal the following year. The United States House of Representatives restricted immigration and the Treaty of Versailles was signed and was later refused ratification by the United States Senate.[12]

Disaster struck the newfound aviation industry after a "windfoot" blimp caught fire and crashed into the Illinois Trust and Savings Bank building in downtown Chicago. Eleven people lost their lives that day on July 22, 1919. The disaster caused an anti-aviation backlash. At an emergency Chicago City Counsel meeting Alderman Anton Cermak (who eventually became Chicago's 35th mayor) introduced an ordinance banning all flights over Chicago. However, the measure failed by one vote.[13]

In May 1919 the *Chicago Herald and Examiner* published an announcement that Universal Pictures in California was running a beauty contest. Joseph Laemmle wrote to his brother Carl in New York reminding him of the beautiful girl he had met five years earlier in Joseph's Chicago neighborhood. Joseph urged Blanche and John Philbin to send Universal a photograph of their daughter Mary.

Although Mary Philbin didn't win the contest (it was won by Gertrude Olmstead) she did get a three-year contract with Universal Pictures. Early in 1920 Mary and her family left for California and Carla was now without her childhood friend.[14]

On March 16, 1920 Carl Laemmle and his business associate Robert H. Cochrane, hired a new general manager of Universal Pictures—Irving Thalberg. It was no secret that a courtship developed between Thalberg and the boss' 18-year-old daughter Rosabelle Laemmle. Rosabelle was pushing Thalberg toward the altar, while Thalberg's mother was against the match. Carl Laemmle felt Thalberg's health problems were so serious, he was concerned his daughter would become a young widow.

Edward Daniel Norton, Carla's maternal grandfather passed away January 29, 1920 at the age of 78 at his Canaan, Connecticut home. Carla never had the opportunity to meet him. Norton named Carla's grandmother Emma Norton in his Last Will and Testament, leaving her $4,000. Prior to her inheritance, Emma sold the Urbana properties that she inherited from her mother, Amelia Loomis (in 1907), and was now on her own. Emma's sister, Carrie Campbell, had relocated to Bethesda, Maryland with daughter, Grace and son-in-law Ralph Danielson. By the summer of 1920, Emma moved to 6121 South Langley in Chicago to be near her family. Mrs. Joseph Laemmle remained devoted to her family and participated in community affairs including her local chapter of the *Daughters of the American Revolution* (known in short as the DAR).[15] Belle supported the League of Women Voters that was founded in Chicago, February 14, 1920.[16] After 42 years the 19th Amendment to the Constitution was ratified Saturday, August 28, granting American women the right to vote. Belle Laemmle, Emogene Loomis, Carrie Loomis Campbell and Grace Danielson were thrilled to see this change during their lifetimes and happy knowing their daughters would have the right to vote.

Carla's 11th birthday on October 20, 1920 would be the last she would celebrate in Chicago. It has been over 80 years since she lived in the windy city and now fondly remembers "snowy winters and varieties of pets," as well as childhood friends including Mary Philbin and Carla's first boyfriend, Scottie Hopper, who had lived on nearby Champlain Avenue. Scottie was 10-year-old Carla's very first love. "Scottie was how I discovered boys. We were about the same age."

Life changing event: Carl Laemmle's letter to his brother, Joseph preparing for their move to California (December 18, 1920).

The Joseph Laemmle family was soon destined for another life-changing event when a letter arrived before Christmas from *Universal Film Manufacturing Co., 1600 Broadway, New York, N.Y.*

The top of the letter read, "December 18, 1920 by Harry H. Zehner, assistant secretary to Carl Laemmle."

> Dear Brother Joe,
> I have a wire from Irving Thalberg in which he notifies me that you can occupy the house at Universal City anytime you are ready. He will furnish the home for you until such time as your own furniture arrives. In the meantime I will get ready and either build a house for you in Hollywood, or nearby, or buy one. Maybe you will like it at Universal City so well that you would not

care to live elsewhere. Of course, it will be a little inconvenient for your child to go to school in Hollywood, provided she does go to school at all. Anyway, these are all minor details, which can be arranged very satisfactorily when you get to California. I told Irving you would be ready to leave in about four weeks.

With love, Your Brother, Carl

Harry Zehner, Carl Laemmle's secretary who typed the 1920 letter to Joseph Laemmle.

Four weeks after receiving the letter—Monday, January 17, 1921 to be exact (Carl Laemmle's 56th birthday)—the family was onboard a train that departed from Dearborn Street Station. Three days later, on Joseph's 67th birthday, they arrived at the Santa Fe Railroad Station in Los Angeles, California. Universal City was located just over the Caheunga Pass from Hollywood—far from Chicago and the concrete jungle of Washington Park.

Universal City would be an exciting wonderland for Carla and her family and would be her home for the next 16 years. Joseph Laemmle, his wife Belle, mother-in-law, Emma Norton and Carla all made the move to this new "land of opportunity."

When Carla was 15 one of her poems were published in a Los Angeles newspaper. Her poem was entitled, *My Land of Dreams*— a place, one could say, that she has lived:

My bed is a magic railroad
Which carries me in my dreams
To many a far-off country,
And to many unknown seas.

I visit the mystic Egypt,
Where the wonderful Sphinx doth stand
Though far off in the desert
Keeps guard o'er all her land

Sometimes I journey to China
And many a secret I know,
About the winding, narrow streets
That aged so long ago.

I go to Magic India
Where the swaying Deodar trees
Bend their necks and chant
Sweet murmurs to the gentle breeze.

So on and on I travel,
And sing and dance and play —
For every living thing is happy
And everyone is gay.

But sometime when I journey forth,
My spirit will go too far
I will not see the familiar Nile
Nor India's pearly shore.

My spirit will commune
With strange Celestial souls,
And to that wondrous throng be joined,
Never to return.

Act One: Scene Two
Beth's Universal Experience
1921-1934

It was a lovely sunny October day when Carla Laemmle's 95th birthday celebration was held at Universal City, California in 2004. As I walked arm in arm with Carla we sang to each other "You are My Sunshine." It was an exciting day—we were VIP guests at Universal City. During the birthday lunch a letter was hand delivered to Carla:

> Dear Miss Laemmle,
> On behalf of Ron Meyer and your friends at Universal Studios, we congratulate you on your 95th birthday. This is a wonderful milestone and one we are very pleased to acknowledge. Your Uncle Carl Laemmle created the distinct legacy our company enjoys today. It is one that our new owners, NBC and General Electric speak of with great respect. We remain the oldest and largest film studio in the world thanks to the vision your Uncle made a reality. We hope you enjoy your very special day and are delighted to welcome you the Universal Studios.
> Sincerely, Susan Fleishman

Among the other guests in the Universal City dining room that day were David Simeur, Michal Kerestes, and special guest Mirko Bayer, who had arrived earlier that week from his home in Laupheim, Germany. Carla reminisced about how Universal Pictures has changed from her early days at the studio. She first discussed her name changes over the years—from Rebekah Laemmle to Beth Laemmle, to Carla Laemmle, and for professional reasons, the name Carol Lenard. She said:

> The name Beth Laemmle must have come about 1924. My mother had a numerologist who thought the name Beth would have good vibrations for me. Well, as time passed, I felt it had no vibration. So when they came up with Carla [in early 1931], I thought that was just a lovely name and

The Universal Experience – (left to right) Michal Kerestes, Mirko Bayer, David Simeur, Sandra R. Williamson, Carla Laemmle and Jeff Pirtle (October 20, 2004, Carla's 95th birthday).

> I liked that. Then for a while, I was Carol Lenard. However, I kept the name Carla Laemmle, although my birth certificate still reads Rebekah Isabelle Laemmle.

To Carla, the first major life change for her was the family move to Universal City, California. As she remembered:

> First and foremost, my uncle Carl had succeeded in persuading his brother Joseph Laemmle, my father, who had long suffered from ill health, to leave the harsh winters of Chicago and move his family out west. It was sunny when we left Chicago and sunny when we arrived in California…As I remember it, it was a long, long train ride.
>
> We moved right into our charming little white bungalow, which had been completely furnished by the studio property department, until our own furniture would arrive from Chicago. Our bungalow was situated some distance away from the road, just back of an enormous block long stretch of beautiful green lawn that reached all the way to a row of towering, pungent smelling petunias bordering the studio side of the wall, which extended the full

length of the lawn. Sweet smelling pepper trees marked the front gate and driveway entrance to the Studio. A four-foot high cement wall separated the studio grounds from the sidewalk.

Even though many years ago, Carla remembers the sights and sounds of the area :

> Around dusk, some of the largest and most beautiful velvety-winged moths that I had ever seen congregated near the foliage. Orange groves covered much of the countryside. They were attracted by the fragrance and nectar. How I loved going outside at sundown. It was a very enchanting time of day for me. Most of the low-lying hills around Universal were still more or less on the wild side and sparsely built up with very few houses. Having come to California from the cement jungle of Chicago, it took me a while to become accustomed to the calling of the coyotes at night, and the roaring of the lions from the back lot zoo, early in the morning, at feeding time.
>
> Among the wildlife that frequented the grounds near the Laemmle bungalow were opossums, gophers, squirrels, owls, bats, lizards, frogs, snakes and skunks—"especially skunks." Among Carla's personal pets was a beautiful collie that got into an unfortunate confrontation with a skunk—there's nothing worse than a wet dog smell, but poor Carla had a wet dog that smelled of skunk.

Little Rebekah at the age of eleven, playing in the huge yard with her dog, Dixie, at Universal City home behind "Old New York Street" set. She always had an array of animals that she loved.

On the studio lot, Carla distinctly remembers Universal's Old New York Street set:

It was a short distance back and to the left of our bungalow. It was a perfect replica, down to the smallest detail. I could almost smell the spicy aroma of corned beef and pickles coming from the storefront delicatessen. To the east of Old New York Street laid an uncultivated area with a rather deep overgrown ravine. During the rainy season, a considerable amount of water flowed through it. A quaint rustic wooden bridge spanned the two sides of the gully. The area on the opposite side of the ravine was used mainly for horticultural purposes. Just beyond the cultivated garden area, many horses and cattle roamed and grazed. A considerable amount of animal droppings accumulated. The combination of manure and moisture provided just the right field for the propagation of mushrooms. One day I found a mushroom the size of a dinner plate. I couldn't believe it! It was the largest I had ever seen. I was accustomed to the smaller-sized button mushrooms. I decided to take it to my friend, Peter the Hermit.

Peter the Hermit was an ageless, bearded, white-haired, Biblical looking figure who lived in a little shack near Universal Studios with his dog and goats. He was a vegetarian, drank goat's milk and ate his vegetables raw. I gave Peter the mushroom and he said it was a real one. He thanked me and chomped it right down.

Carl remembers Peter as a colorful personality and a celebrity of sorts. He would often be seen staff in hand, briskly striding along Hollywood Boulevard, hailing one and all in his booming voice. In the book *Mae West "it ain't no sin"* by Simon Louvish, the author writes that in an interview in the *New York World-Telegram* in 1933 that Mae West said the only man she wanted to meet in Hollywood was Peter the Hermit. His real name was Peter Howard and *The Story of Hollywood* by Gregory Paul Williams states, "he was, in his prime, a strikingly handsome, muscular man....Hollywood's most famous ascetic, he lived with pet greyhounds and burros in a tent on a vacant Laurel Canyon lot."

Carla always had a love of animals and before leaving Chicago she was worried that California might not have any animals. She remembers

Introducing Rebekah Laemmle, dancer, age 12, Universal City, California (1921).

that her father assured her that "there would be plenty of pets where we were going…and he was right!"

> The most outstanding attraction for me at Universal was the Zoo! It too was located on Universal's "backlot" about a mile or so from the main studio buildings, which was also home to scores of horses, sheep, goats, lions, tigers,

a giraffe, a couple of elephants, monkeys, a specially trained chimpanzee, a variety of exotic birds and a camel named Houdini. I named the camel Houdini because he managed to extricate himself from being tethered by the zookeeper. I managed to serendipitously entice him with a bowl of oats every time he would get away from the backlot, to our front lawn. The trek was about a mile and a half.

Strange as it sounds, at Universal there was actually a working chicken farm that was located on the backlot. It seems Universal City was formerly a poultry ranch. Carla remembers that the farm became something of a joke:

> It wasn't the best investment my uncle had there. It did have a lot of chickens there and a lot of eggs. Admission price for the tour was 25 cents. For an extra nickel, eggs were given to the spectators in small baskets, if they chose.

The studios tours began when Universal opened, but they were discontinued after the arrival of the talkies. The Universal Studio tours did not resume until 1964 and continue to this day.

Along with the chickens, there were many horses on the lot for Carla to admire. One of her favorite four-legged creatures was Trixie, the Laughing Show Horse. Trixie's claim to fame was as the star of the 1926 short *Whoa, Emma!* The Winnipeg Free Press on August 24, 1935 reported that Trixie was given 16 dye treatments to turn her into a platinum blonde for a Harold Lloyd movie *The Milky Way*. Unfortunately, no other mention could be found of Trixie's Hollywood career. Carla recalls:

> Trixie was really an exceptionally smart horse. She would perform on command any one of her repertoire of tricks: sit on her haunches, play dead, roll over, whinny a horselaugh raising her lips, shake hands, rear up and paw the air, or count out a number by pawing the ground. She could also sashay around and dance a little jig. She appeared in many movies with stars like Harry Langdon.

Rebekah's first annual costume/birthday party at Universal City, age 12. Trixie the Laughing Show Horse was a guest along with students from Ernest Belcher's ballet school.

Mr. Raleigh J. Malchow was Trixie's owner and trainer. He worked at Universal as a stuntman. Carla said:

> He was a true cowboy in every sense of the word. He lived across Lankershim Boulevard, which was across from Universal. I had never ridden a horse before, but Mr. Malchow taught me how to ride Trixie bareback and to perform tricks with her; it was great fun for me. I loved her so.

One day Malchow came over and explained to Carla's mother that he had to settle his late uncle's estate in Kansas and had to be away for two or three months. He asked Mrs. Laemmle if it was possible that he borrow $100 so he could make the trip to Kansas. She readily agreed. Mr. Malchow then asked if Carla could care for Trixie while he was gone. Mrs. Laemmle agreed and Carla was thrilled with the idea. She remembered:

> Thus, I became the horse sitter for the next three months. I set Trixie up in one of the garages and saw that she had

plenty of water and hay that I bought at a nearby feed store. For exercise, I rode her around Universal. I think she enjoyed it as much as I did.

When Malchow returned, he immediately paid Mrs. Laemmle back the $100 he had borrowed and even reimbursed Carla for the hay. It was hard for her to part with Trixie. However, Carla would still get to see Trixie and even occasionally ride her. Carla remembered a tragic day later in the early 1930s. She said:

> It was devastating when I learned how Trixie died. As I recall, these young hoodlums who hung out and around in the area, gave her a bucket of freshly mixed cement, which she ate. I am grateful to have the pictures of me with Trixie.

Across the road from the Joseph Laemmle house, on what had once been El Camino Real, was Campo de Cahuenga, one of the the most historic landmarks in California. It was there on January 16, 1847, that U.S. Army Colonel John Fremont and General Andres Pico signed the Treaty of Cahuenga, ceding California to the United States.

The Daughters of the American Revolution, of which Belle Laemmle was an active member, held their meetings there. She helped to organize the Peyton Randolph Chapter (Campo de Cahuenga) at Universal City.[1]

Carla had the following to say about her immediate family during this time:

> My mother spent many long hours at the library. Anytime one couldn't find my mother, the library was the most likely place she would be. She also belonged to several other social groups throughout her life. When I look back on my father's health. I really don't think that he would have made it through another horrendous winter in Chicago had it not been for my uncle. However, my father did work for my uncle as his West Coast Representative with Universal Pictures, Incorporated. And, the Gods of Karma were good to my father by keeping him with us in California the first eight years. He passed away in 1929.

I recall taking his death philosophically. He had been in such poor health, most of his life. I loved my father. He was a good businessman and I am proud of what he did for his family. My mother loved California. She was astute when it came to my learning how to dance. She was a wonderful cook and my father showed her how to cook some German dishes. She remained devoted to my father until his death. In fact, I have treasured the following article that was written by my mother. It tells so much about her genial personality and her marriage to my father. It was published in a Chicago newspaper before we made the move west.

The article reads as follows:

Mrs. Joseph Laemmle,
Secretary of the Chicago Alumnae Association,
University of Illinois...

A man who would be perfect to one woman might from the standpoint of another be unbearable. Happiness, like perfection is a relative term, it means something different to every individual. In my own case my husband is perfect to me, because he satisfies me with every particular. We are congenial—a compliment one to the other. And we still are in the land of romance. In most homes there is too little romance. Life becomes too mater-of-fact.

I do not believe that even the H.C.L. and the many complexities of modern living should prevent a husband and wife from living in tune with the earlier ideals of love. My husband and I are congenial yet we are of different nationalities and racial characteristics. His viewpoints from education and early environment are essentially different from mine. But in spite of these variants that might seem to lead the way to friction we are in perfect accord. There is a little philosophy of my own to which I wish to give expression in this bit of a testimonial to the genuine goodness of my husband. No man should be made to feel the marriage fetters or forced to curtail his freedom or liberty to express his personality, as he desires.

Belle Laemmle (celebrates her 40th year with fellow members of the Peyton Randolph Chapter of the Daughters of the American Revolution (Los Angeles, 1944).

> No wife should look upon herself as a reformer—of her own or other husbands. If there were fewer wives of that kind there would be more husbands attaining the so-called standard of perfection. Many women make their husbands feel too much married.

Of her maternal grandmother Emogene Loomis Norton, Carla remembers:

> She was such a dear person. She was never a hard woman to please and she had such a loving disposition. I loved her so. She always called me Rebekah! To this day I can hear her voice calling "WHERE'S REBEKAH"? She gave me my first bible when I was 12. My grandmother had a great rapport with my Uncle Carl. They had a great deal of love and respect for each other.

While still school age, Carla's days were spent working with her private tutor and three days a week she met with her ballet instructor Mr. Belcher. She appeared occasionally at the Hollywood Bowl in Belcher's ballet vignettes.

Beth's 15th birthday (1924). Guests included her father Joseph Laemmle (second row- fourth from left) sitting beside the birthday girl and her friend Mary Philbin, John and Blanche Philbin, Mary's parents are seated on the ground (far left). Seated at ground level sixth from the left is Paul Kohner, a favorite of Uncle Carl's, who later became a successful producer and entertainment agent. Cousin Robert Wyler is in soldier's uniform (top right).

Ernest Belcher was a well-respected dance choreographer and he and his student became good friends. Born in London, England, Thursday, June 8, 1882, Mr. Belcher studied ballet in London and was the principal danseur at the Alhambra Theatre. He came to Los Angeles in 1915 and founded the Celeste School of Dance in 1916, which supplied dancers for films. He also produced ballets for Hollywood Bowl concerts from 1923-1936. His career took off in 1918 when he staged dances for D.W. Griffith's *Broken Blossoms*. He was a trainer and coach to many performers including Pola Negri, Ramon Navarro, Mary Pickford, Nanette Fabray and Shirley Temple as well as his own daughter Marge Celeste Belcher. Dance fans will know Marge as part of the famous dancing duo Marge and Gower Champion. She and Gower Champion worked together and then married. Their presence brightened many Hollywood films including 1951's *Showboat*. Ernest Belcher passed away in Hollywood, California, Saturday, February 24, 1973.

Carla's birthday celebrations were always a special event in her life and those held during those Universal days were especially fun:

> Since my birthday ran close to Halloween, there would become birthday/costume parties. From the age of 12 to 16 as you see by the photographs, we celebrated and had fun. Even Trixie attended one!! I remember Sylvia Thalberg as being one of my friends from that early period. She was the sister of Irving Thalberg. They were all filmed.[2] Many of my invited friends were made up of actors and members of my Ernest Belcher dancing

class or relatives somehow. My fourteenth birthday was most memorable. I had previously discovered that fringe benefits came naturally with the territory of being Carl Laemmle's niece. I simply made a call to the Universal Property Department and asked them to please set up some real scary Halloween for my party, and Voila! Did they ever do it! They rigged the narrow tree-lined lane with all manner of weird and spooky gimmicks and created a special effects horror masterpiece, complete with eerie lighting and sound effects. It proved all too much for my young dancer friend, Dorothy Weigal. When a life-sized, bone rattling skeleton suddenly jumped out at her from behind a tree, she gave a piercing scream and fainted dead away! A whiff of smelling salts promptly revived her, the only casualty of the evening!

Universal City had it's own post office, Mayor, police and fire departments as well as a hospital—complete with a resident doctor and nurse. Universal also had it's own school, but Carla did not attend classes there, she had a private tutor in downtown Hollywood.

After the family arrived at Universal, Carla learned that she had a half-brother who was 22-years her senior, Edward Laemmle. He was hired by his uncle Carl in 1915 and was a successful director and producer of mostly Westerns at Universal City. He was 33 years old and married. During the 1921-22 season, Edward Laemmle had an amazing 25 films released to theaters. Laemmle directed mostly Western shorts but also directed features including *Hey! Hey! Cowboy* (1927) with Hoot Gibson and *The Texas Bad Man* (1932) with Tom Mix.

Nepotism was a standard tradition at Universal City—there were nearly 70 relatives on the payroll including: nephew Ernst Laemmle (like Edward, Ernst directed mostly Western shorts

Edward Laemmle, Carla's half brother. He was nearly 22 years older than Carla.

Among the Rugged Peaks

but also directed features such as *The Grip of the Yukon* [1928] with Francis X. Bushman and is credited as an assistant writer on Preston Sturges' *Sullivan's Travels* [1941], nephews Arthur Alexander (producer of mostly B Westerns and mysteries including *The Whispering Skull* [1944] with Tex Ritter and *Queen of Burlesque* with Evelyn Ankers [1946] and his brother Max Alexander (producer of mostly B Westerns and mysteries including *The Shadow Strikes* [1937] with Rod La Rocque as Lamont Cranston, the Shadow and *Death Rides the Range* [1939] with Ken Maynard, his wife Shirley left him for Edgar G. Ulmer), Nat Ross (a.k.a. Nathaniel R. Ross, another nephew, who directed many Western shorts as well as a few features including *The Galloping Kid* [1922] with Hoot Gibson; he was murdered when an ex-employee shot him in the heart) and William Wyler and his brother Robert Wyler. Laemmle also believed in supporting his friends as well as his family. Working at Universal could also be found many immigrant acquaintances such as Paul Kohner (producer on *Cat and the Canary* [1927], *The Man Who Laughs* [1928] and associate producer on *Dracula*) Kurt Neumann (prolific writer/director/producer whose resume includes *The Secret of the Blue Room* [1933], *Rocketship X-M* [1950] and *The Fly* [1958] and was originally considered for director of *Bride of Frankenstein*) Paul Leni (director of *The Cat and the Canary* and *The Man Who Laugh*s and *The Last Warning* [1929]) and Joseph Levigard (directed many Western shorts for Universal).

Regarding her half-brother, Edward Laemmle, Carla remembered:

> I adored him. He was a fine director, very accomplished, and a wonderful human being. I loved him, but I did not

know until we came out to California that I had a half-brother. In 1923, after we were already living in California, Eddie married Peppi Heller of Ichenhausen, Germany. Peppi's older sister Frieda, had previously married Louis Laemmle. [It was a good many years earlier that the young Carl Laemmle was engaged by the Heller family to work at their busy little wholesale-retail novelty establishment in Ichenhausen. Thus at the age of 13, Carl Laemmle began serving his 3-year apprenticeship, learning the art of the trade and a smattering of English.] Peppi and Eddie had two children, Carlotta and Conni. When they grew older I would drive over to their house and give them dancing lessons. Eddie and Peppi also invited me to the scrumptious dinners that they prepared, mostly on Sunday nights. Then one terrible night in 1937, as the family was sitting around the dinner table having dinner, tragedy struck. Suddenly, without warning, Edward suffered a massive heart attack and collapsed. He died within minutes. The suddenness of it all was devastating. He was so young. He was to turn 50 that year and had so much to live for. I shall always remember Eddie with deepest affection. I am grateful to have had him in my life for 16 years.[3]

World events and new technologies were changing Hollywood as well as the nation, and living in Hollywood, Carla was right there in the midst. Film comedian, producer and director Charlie Chaplin made his first full-length film, *The Kid* in 1921 for First National. The silent film starred Chaplin as A Tramp and child actor Jackie Coogan as The Kid—it was a run away hit.

Also in 1921, in Kansas City, Missouri a young artist, who would later work briefly for Carl Laemmle before becoming a worldwide legend, started his first job at the Kansas City Slide Company—his name was Walt Disney.[4]

This was the era of Anything Goes as girls raised their skirts and bobbed their hair. "The Roaring Twenties" began with the well-meaning but short-sighted Anti-Saloon League and the Women's Christian Temperance Union forced Prohibition upon an unwilling public. The women behind the temperance leagues were trying to curb wife beating and child abuse, but the behind the scenes machinations were provided by industrialists who felt alcohol could affect worker's productivity. This unpopular law forced upon the unsuspecting citizens created a boondoggle of mind-boggling proportions and spawned speakeasies, bootlegging and gangsters. While speakeasies and gangsters didn't really affect Hollywood until the late 1920s,[5] Tinseltown did have more than their fair share of scandals.[6]

In 1921, newspapers were blazing the sensational headlines when popular silent film comedian Roscoe "Fatty" Arbuckle was arrested and charged with the murder of starlet Virginia Rappe after a wild three day party. The papers reported he crushed her with his weight and/or raped her. The reporting had little to do with the true facts of the death. While the media had him convicted, Arbuckle was acquitted after three lurid trials. While Arbuckle was found innocent, his career never recovered. In 1922 another Hollywood murder rocked the fledgling movie industry when director William Desmond Taylor was found in his apartment shot in the back. Taylor was trying to help Hollywood beauty, actress Mabel Normand kick booze and dope. Several authors theorize Taylor was killed because of his strong opposition to drug dealers, but he was also stalked by an infatuated lover, who was also a suspect. To this day, the murder of William Desmond Taylor remains unsolved. Another unsolved and scandalous murder was the mysterious death of movie producer Thomas Ince in 1924. Ince and a distinguished list of companions including Charlie Chaplin, Marion Davies and Louella Parsons were aboard William Randolph Hurst's yacht celebrating Ince's birthday. In 2001 Peter Bogdanovich made a fictionalized film of the murder, *The Cat's Meow* starring Kirsten Dunst as Marion Davies and Cary Elwes as Ince. [7]

Director Erich von Stroheim (wearing white gloves), on the set of *Foolish Wives* at Universal 1922. Joseph Laemmle, the director's friend is pictured in the 2nd row to the extreme left.

Carl Laemmle mixed a taste of European culture with a completely Americanized acceptance of Westerns, suspense and sports serials as "sure-fire box-office." Another type of film was also all the rage at that time—the "socially conscious" a.k.a. exploitation film. "Six Reels of Thrilling Realities" was the tagline used for *Traffic in Souls* released by Universal in 1913. The film concerned a young woman, who along with her policeman boyfriend, searches for her missing sister. The sister was kidnapped after having an unchaperoned date. She was captured by white slavers and forced into prostitution. *Traffic in Souls* was the first movie to be booked simultaneously in 30 New York City theatres. Other titles of the same ilk included *The Bride's Awakening*, *The Model's Confession* and *Mortgaged Wife*.

It was during this period that an Austrian by the name of Erich von Stroheim introduced himself to Carl Laemmle. Laemmle was impressed by von Stroheim and gave him his first U.S. job as a director on *Blind Husbands*. Von Stroheim not only directed the film, he wrote it and starred as well. Erich von Stroheim had an intriguing life and career in Hollywood. Film buffs will remember him as the butler Max von Mayerling in *Sunset Blvd* (Paramount, 1950) The role would earn him an Academy Award nomination for Supporting Actor, and although he didn't win, he did pick up a Golden Globe for the role.

During this Golden Age of Hollywood, movie moguls were hard-working immigrants who clawed their way to the top, but never forgot their roots. During difficult economic times they were smart enough to realize the public needed exciting, fantastic movies filled with beautiful costumes, locations and people. Clothes worn by popular actresses like Clara Bow and Joan Crawford were instantly imitated. Movie magazines featured actors such as Rudolf Valentino and Douglas Fairbanks, Sr. But it was the comedians who really got the country laughing again—Buster Keaton, Harry Langdon and Harold Lloyd were all the rage. However, the most popular of the comedians, and one of Carla's favorites, was Charlie Chaplin. Carl Laemmle once considered making a deal with Chaplin, but the star declined. Another huge Hollywood star was also a favorite of Carla—Rin Tin Tin, the amazing German Shepherd that became Hollywood's first canine star.

Carl Laemmle Jr. and Julius Bernheim soon after Mr. Bernheim's arrival to America (1920). Bernheim would later become general manager of Universal after Irving Thalberg's departure in 1923.

Irving Thalberg had writer/director credits on six films in November 1922 when this issue of Universal City News hit the stands. Irving Thalberg wrote the following entitled LAEMMLE LUCK:

Those who have differed with Universal's policy in picture-making; those who have disagreed with Universal's judgment of stars and stories are attributing the splendid success of our product to "Laemmle Luck." "They are quite right." "It is the same "LAEMMLE LUCK" that enabled Carl Laemmle to build the world's greatest motion picture organization from a standing start with nothing to go on except genius, mixed with brains. "It is the same "LAEMMLE LUCK" that kept Universal City the white-spot on the motion picture map while other producers were beating their cameras into stock shares and sloughing a furrow to Wall Street. "It was "LAEMMLE LUCK" that reorganized the entire motion picture business on the live-and-let-live basis. It was "LAEMMLE LUCK" that blazed a trail across the trackless immensity of the industry's future to make the way easier for those who follow him. "LAEMMLE LUCK" has made the Universal Emblem the Pride-Mark of the motion picture industry. It is keeping 19 companies going today and carrying 1700 men and women on the payroll. The world is backing "LAEMMLE LUCK" to win every point that makes the motion picture industry bigger and cleaner and finer. You are vitally in the game at Universal City. LEAD WITH YOUR HEART!

In February 1923 Irving Thalberg, resigned his post at Universal to produce movies for L.B. Mayer at Louis B. Mayer Productions. Thalberg was passionate about bringing the Gaston Leroux novel *The Phantom of the Opera* to the silver screen and as its star the amazing Lon Chaney and had acquired the rights for Universal. Carl Laemmle reportedly said, "That ungrateful little bastard is leaving me with a million dollar picture that has a misshapen freak as the main character!" Thalberg would be sorely missed by the studio—*The Phantom of the Opera* production was a nightmare from beginning to end.

The romance between Thalberg and Rosabelle was also off. This news became rather public at the time. Thalberg would later marry actress and MGM star Norma Shearer on September 29, 1927. And Rosabelle Laemmle would later marry Mark Stanley Bergerman on January 2, 1929.

Soon after his daughter's marriage, Carl Laemmle appointed his new son-in-law as production supervisor at Universal. Bergerman produced numerous pictures between 1930 and 1935, as well as over 100 short subject and sports documentaries.

After Thalberg's departure from Universal, the position of general manager was given to Uncle Carl's nephew Julius Bernheim.

Erich Von Stroheim's obsession with detail that caused many delays and eventually cost the actor/director his job at Universal. He never directed another movie for Universal after *Merry-Go-Round* (1923)—a production that was literally pulled out from under him and Rupert Julian was credited as director. Julian would be given the plum job of directing *The Phantom of the Opera*, which he promptly made more of a mess than von Stroheim (Laemmle had originally wanted him to direct the story) could have ever accomplished. Von Stroheim and Joseph Laemmle were friends during this time. Carla remembers:

> Von Stroheim was a perfectionist in everything he did, a great director and a great actor. I, later, had the great fortune to have him direct me in a screen test. He was a stickler for authenticity. He even insisted on having

real lace on the ladies undergarments. His penchant for spending much money on minor details ired my uncle. In spite of Von Stroheim's genius, Uncle Carl fired him! I thought that Von Stroheim was quite a sexy man. He'd come over to the house and played cards with my father and others that included Julius Bernheim. The only thing that irritated me is that they were all smoking cigars. When my father passed away, I remember that a huge wreath of flowers was sent from Von Stroheim that read *"Auf Wiedersehen."*

Carla remembered her very first *"big"* crush occurred when she learned to drive an automobile at the age of 14. The car she used to learn to drive belonged to Dr. Talatt Nardini, who worked at the Universal City Hospital. Remembering her first infatuation and the doctor who was the object of it, she says, "It was just an innocent thing. I thought that he was the most handsome man I had ever seen in my life, but it was only a crush." Carla was still writing constantly and her father sent a sample of her work to Florence Wilson, who was a critic and reviewer for Universal Pictures. Joseph Laemmle received the following letter from Ms. Wilson dated June 11, 1925:

> My dear Mr. Laemmle, I want to thank you for giving me the little verses of your daughter's to read. In my opinion she is a little genius, or near to that. I have read the little verses she composed at her sixth birthday, and think they are very clever. The later poem is very good too. The verses are of course crude, but talent is there and enough of it to warrant some attention being paid to it, in placing her under proper teachers in order to teach the technique of writing poetry. She has the natural gift and only needs guidance to be very successful I should say. As I have said, the little verses are crude, but the beautiful thought behind these verses is what is very important. With a little thought and help, so far as "the mechanics of writing is concerned, I think this last little poem would be a very good one and worth printing [My Land of Dreams]. Considering the young girl's age [15], it is worthy of attention as it is. Your

daughter is very talented and were she my child I would have these improved to the best advantage. She is quite a remarkable little character dancer. I was surprised when I found she was so young, for she did work on the stage that evening out at the Studio that would have been a credit to a much older artist... ....I notice the name of Mary Philbin. Then you people must have known her for some time. She is a dear little girl. If you happen to see her in her new role you will be astonished I know, for she is almost unrecognizable. She is simply a fright. With kindest regards and thanking you again for giving me these verses and article to read, I am, with lots of good wishes for the little Poetess, and don't let people spoil her by flattery, please.

Very sincerely yours, (Mrs.) Florence Wilson

September 6, 1925 Carl Laemmle premiered in New York *The Phantom of the Opera* starring Lon Chaney. Chaney's co-star was none other than Carla's childhood friend Mary Philbin, who played Christine. Laem-

Beth Laemmle. Prima Ballerina, front and center, *The Phantom of the Opera* (Universal, 1925).

mle had hired Carla's dance instructor Ernest Belcher to choreograph the ballet sequences seen in the film at the Paris Opera House. For the film Belcher chose his 16-year-old prodigy Carla Laemmle, known during this period of her life as Beth. She played the prima ballerina in her motion picture debut in *Phantom of the Opera*. Today, she remains as the only surviving cast member of *The Phantom of the Opera*.

At the age of 16 Carla blossomed into womanhood. She continued to study with Ernest Belcher as well as performing ballet in films that Belcher choreographed. Carla's film ballets include *La Boheme*, *Don Juan* and *Camille*. Carla became acquainted with Willon Fields during this time. Willon's major interest in motion pictures was makeup. Carla remembers that Willon's work was amazing. He could transform himself much like the man of a thousand faces Lon Chaney.

> Willon and I were good friends. He was close to my entire family as a matter of fact. I remember when my cousin, Grace Danielson and her husband Ralph came to Universal in 1926 with my Aunt Carrie Campbell. It was Willon who acted as their tour guide.

A Laemmle Family Picture in Hollywood (1926), Left to right: Louis Laemmle, Mrs. Joseph (Belle) Laemmle, Rosabelle Laemmle, Joseph Laemmle, Siegfried Laemmle, Walter Laemmle, Mrs. Siegfried (Betty) Laemmle, and Ernst Laemmle with Carl Laemmle and "Junior" (seated).

Beth with good friend and fellow actor, Willon Fields at the Shrine Light Opera stage door Willon later became a makeup artist with Warner Bros. Carla never knew what became of her friend Willon or his wife.

Willon Fields and Carla Laemmle lost touch with each other many years ago. His only film credits for makeup include *Desert Vigilante* (1949, uncredited), *Stranger on Horseback* (1955), *Around the World in 80 Days* (1956, uncredited) and *Shake, Rattle & Rock* (1956).

In 1924, Irving Thalberg's new studio Louis B. Mayer Productions merged Metro Pictures and (Samuel) Goldwyn Pictures to form Metro-Goldwyn-Mayer (MGM).

At Universal, Carl Laemmle's son Julius, forever known as Junior, was learning the business from his father.

Junior wished to follow in his father's footsteps and set his sights on the production side. As a result, the teenager successfully wrote, cast and supervised the Universal Junior Jewell series *The Collegians*.

In 1927 Carla made a screen appearance as the flying angel in *Topsy and Eva*, which was released by United Artists Company, newly formed by Mary Pickford, Charlie Chaplin and Douglas Fairbanks. Its director was Del Lord.[8]

The year 1927 set audiences abuzz, literally with movies that spoke! Warner Bros. released the first talkie *The Jazz Singer*, which astounded audiences when popular Vaudevillian Al Jolson sang on film. The movie opened at Grauman's Chinese Theatre where Klieg lights were used for the first time.[9] Universal Pictures would be the last to jump on the sound bandwagon.

December 27, 1927 producer Florenz Ziegfeld opened Oscar Hammerstein's and Jerome Kern's revolutionary hit musical *Showboat* at the

Los Angeles Train Station 1927 – Carl Laemmle greets nephew, Walter Laemmle as he arrives in America. Also to join were (from left to right), Beth Laemmle and her mother Belle.

Among the Rugged Peaks

1928 Shrine Light Opera program showcasing Beth Laemmle in *Sally*.

Ziegfeld Theater.[10] The show would run for 575 performances. Universal would release a partial sound version of the film in 1929 and James Whale would direct an all-star version released in 1936 that starred Irene Dunne and Paul Robeson.

Back in Hollywood, the Academy of Motion Picture Arts and Sciences was founded in Los Angeles that same year.[11]

At 18, Carla auditioned for the Shrine Light Opera and won Premiere Danseuse and began working Monday, December 26, 1927 at the Shrine Civic Auditorium in Los Angeles.

Friday, February 24, 1928 Carla Laemmle opened as the Prima Ballerina in *Sally*. Unfortunately Carla's father Joseph Laemmle was unable to attend because some months earlier he had been placed in a sanitarium. However her mother Belle and her Uncle Carl were present. During Carla's eight-week engagement at the Shrine Civic Auditorium, she appeared in *The Merry Widow, Wildflower, Boccaccio, Naughty Marietta, Prince of Pilsen, No, No, Nanette* and *The Chocolate Soldier*. Press reviews were glowing! The *Los Angeles Examiner* stated, "Beth Laemmle made an instantaneous hit. She is a lovely girl in the face and form and her talents invite praiseworthy adjectives." The *Los Angeles Times* wrote, "Beth Laemmle, the beautiful master of the Ballet, shows great technique in her toe dance." *Los Angeles Evening Herald* said, "Famous dancer wins fame. She won the house with her exquisite dancing." *California Staats-Zeitung* writes, "Beth

Laemmle is a genius. She is the living expression of the Oriental symbolic dances."

In June 1928, Carla Laemmle signed a long-term contract with Universal Pictures. Carla was also accepted as a member of the *Daughters of the American Revolution*, which made her mother just as proud.

Carla's first movie appearance at Universal was as a maid in the comedy/melodrama *The Gate Crasher* starring Patsy Ruth Miller. This was a screen test of sorts to see how well Carla carried herself on screen.

While Wall Street was crashing and Walt Disney and Mickey Mouse were on their way to becoming legends, Carla Laemmle was working as a professional dancer and actress, and as such would be photographed countless times and do numerous screen tests. Carla was flattered when Universal loaned her out to MGM in 1929 to work as a dancer in *The Broadway Melody of 1929*. It was an Irving Thalberg production, co-produced by Thalberg's brother-in-law Lawrence Weingarten and starring Charles King, Anita Page (who passed away September 6, 2008 at the age of 98) and Bessie Love.

It was later learned that Carla's scene had been cut from the released print. Two photographs Carla kept from the dance number are all that remain. Had the footage survived, we would see a huge oyster shell emerging from the floor. Carla made her entrance from the shell onto the floor to perform "The Pearl Ballet," alongside a group of women from the Albertina Rasch ballet. Carla recalls:

Beth's opening night in Los Angeles, at the Shrine with Uncle Carl Laemmle (1928).

Beth Laemmle in her movie debut playing a maid in *The Gate Crasher* with Glenn Tryon and Patsy Ruth Miller (Universal, 1928).

> What I did was step out from this huge oyster shell. I was in a skin colored leotard [The costumes were made by Erté.] So, I walked out of the oyster shell and did my dance center stage. After my dance, I went back into the shell and it closed.

Recently in 2008, Carla was invited by friends to a film showing. She was delighted to see herself emerge from the shell and watch the entire musical dance routine she had done 80 years ago! What Carla didn't realize was that she had just watched a different MGM movie that was also released in 1929—*The Hollywood Revue of 1929*. *The Hollywood Revue of 1929* showcased a huge variety of stars that included Charles King, Bessie Love (both of whom previously starred in *Broadway Melody*) Joan Crawford, Norma Shearer, John Gilbert, Marion Davies, Stan Laurel and Oliver Hardy, all playing themselves. The masters of ceremonies were Jack Benny and Conrad Nagel.

Carla went uncredited in her only number, "Programme 2nd Part: Tableau of Jewels." Her dance was proceeded by "The Dance of the

First of two photos that Carla kept over the years from the mysteriously deleted "oyster shell" scene from *The Broadway Melody* that somehow ended up in *The Hollywood Revue* (MGM, 1929).

Beth comes out of her shell and dances. Her deleted scene turned out to be included in MGM's *Hollywood Revue of 1929*. The number was entitled "Tableau of Jewels" with the accompaniment of the Albertina Rasch ballet.

Sea" a sequel-type comedy skit by comedian Buster Keaton. How Carla's deleted scene moved from *The Broadway Melody of 1929* into *The Hollywood Revue of 1929* remains a mystery, but since MGM was using the *Hollywood Revue* to introduce America to the sound of their favorite movie stars talking and singing, Thalberg probably figured why let a good dance number go to waste. Of course the footage could have just gotten mixed up.

Both movies were successful at the box office. In fact, *The Broadway Melody of 1929* earned three million dollars, was MGM's first sound film and became the first full-sound film to win the Academy Award for Best Picture.[12]

On a professional level Carla's life was going well. But on a personal level, her family would face some grim news. On Friday, March 22, 1929, Carla's mother Belle received a phone call from the Glendale Sanitarium. As Carla remembers:

> My mother and I arrived there not long after noon. There was my father. He was sitting straight up. It appeared

that he was eating his lunch when, in fact, my father had passed away. He is buried at the Jewish cemetery, outside the mausoleum where my uncle and his family are interred.

At Universal, on Carl Laemmle, Jr.'s 21st birthday his father appointed him general manager in charge of all productions. Junior's brother-in-law Stanley Bergerman shared his thoughts with this writer in 1997:

> To have two brilliant, productive individuals in one family, and having given volumes of distinctive films, is indeed a rarity. I am appreciative for being in the family.

He also commented on Junior Laemmle in 1996 by saying:

> He did well with the horror pictures, much to his father's disapproval. But Junior thought that he knew what his public wanted and he proved right. He was the first to make it a form of art in sound pictures.

Junior had a flair for big-budget productions. To him one outstanding production should follow another. His extravagant business practices and his personal penchant for gambling eventually lead to Junior Laemmle's professional decline. But that would be in the near future. At this point in his young life, Junior was earning praise for his vision, specifically one film—*All Quiet on the Western Front*. Adapted to the screen from the best-selling WWI novel by Erich Maria Remarquet, the film became the first major anti-war movie of the sound era. *All Quiet on the Western Front* began shooting on Universal's backlot

Last photo of Mr. And Mrs. Joseph Laemmle, on his 74th birthday, January 20, 1929.

Among the Rugged Peaks

in November 1929. Junior Laemmle was head of production though his father oversaw most of the project. Carla remembered:

> Universal reconstructed the hills on the back lot into the battlefields that you see in the movie. I felt as if I was seeing history being made. It was an immediate hit and won the Academy Award for Best Picture of 1930. What I remember most about the filming of *All Quiet on the Western Front* is that I had a crush on Lew Ayres at the time! I remember watching him from a far, as filming was taking place. I never met him, but I thought he was such a handsome man. The prestige of *All Quiet on the Western Front* was such that it went down in film history as one of the most important motion pictures ever made. It was also on the backlot where I remember having seen, long before *All Quiet*, the spectacular fire scene in *Foolish Wives* that was successfully filmed in one take! And I saw much of the filming of *The Hunchback of Notre Dame* with Lon Chaney in his horrifically remarkable makeup as Quasimodo. I understand that the hump on his back weighed 20 pounds! I watched him walk and maneuver himself around in scenes being shot a complete replica of the lower half of Notre Dame's great French cathedral, on Universal's backlot. I understand that an unfortunate fire later destroyed the cathedral in the 1960s.

By the late-1920s the major Hollywood movie studios had been formed and were doing big business at the box office. Besides Universal, they included Paramount, Metro-Goldwyn-Mayer, Columbia Pictures. Warner Bros. and Fox Film Corporation (later known beginning in 1935 as 20th Century Fox). Each studio became known for a specific genre or type of film. At Universal it would become the horror film, which to this day still brings them in hefty dollars.

With the success of MGM's *The Broadway Melody of 1929*. Junior Laemmle decided Universal should dip their toes into the musical pool. He produced a musical picture called *Broadway* that was rather successful for Universal. It was adapted from a play by George Abbott about two nightclub dancers, who were accidentally involved with bootleggers and murder. This would be Universal's first all-talkie with color sequences.

The film came out in two versions, talking and silent. The silent print had been thought lost, but a complete film was recently discovered in Hungary.

Broadway was one of four Universal movies directed by Hungarian Paul Fejos (Pál Fejös) in association with Carl Laemmle, Jr. A biography of Fejos on Hollywood.com states he was a set designer and director, who made several films in Budapest before he moved to the U.S. in 1923. From 1924-1926 he worked as a bacteriologist at the Rockefeller Institute before moving to California where he made a low-budget film that gained the attention of Laemmle. Fejos and Junior Laemmle became friends and in no time at all Fejos was directing films produced by Carl Laemmle, Jr. Unfortunately, this friendship is said to have been the precursor to Junior's serious germ phobia.

Carla Laemmle would go from MGM back to Universal to appear in *King of Jazz*.

Father and son Laemmle, as well as American radio listeners were huge fans of bandleader Paul Whiteman and His Orchestra. *King of Jazz* would star Whiteman and showcase spectacular production numbers in addition to comedy sketches, as well as individual song and dance novelties. This production included the talents of danseur, Beth Laemmle. Carla remembers:

> I was in three numbers, "Melting Pot," where I performed a tarantella. I was also doing a few dance turns in the "Finale Number." However, my favorite dance number from *King of Jazz* was dancing on this huge piano during George Gershwin's "Rhapsody in Blue."[13]

Beth Laemmle in one of her three sequences from *King of Jazz* (Universal, 1930).

King of Jazz also marked the film debut of a crooner who was then part of a trio known as The Rhythm Boys. His name was Bing Crosby. Al Rinker and Harry Barris were the other members of the trio featured in the film.[14] The box office draw of *King of Jazz* unfortunately did not meet with its public.

Some months following the releases of these musicals was a day living in infamy. Thursday, October 24, 1929, better known as Black Thursday. The New York stock market took a steep downward crash. By Tuesday, October 29, the United States Stock Market had bottomed out, thus, began the Great United States Depression.

Before the end of the 1920s, world events included President Calvin Coolidge finishing his two terms in office. Herbert C. Hoover then became the new President of the United States.

King of Jazz was another of Carla's " fortunate life experiences." She met some of the most interesting people during the shooting of the movie. The people of whom Carla remembers best are Helen and James Dietrich.[15]

King of Jazz (Universal, 1930) Beth Laemmle was billed in this extravaganza of song and dance, originally filmed in color. During rehearsals, Beth sits on the piano as George Gershwin is seated and Billy Rose stands by.

Helen and Jimmy Dietrich played a big part in my early life at Universal as well as over the years. I met Jimmy Dietrich during the filming of *King of Jazz*. He was the Musical Director at Universal at the time and a most gifted musician and composer. He and his wife, Helen Dietrich, likewise a fine musician, were to become my very close and loving friends over the many happy years ahead. Helen, also, was an accomplished concert pianist, [who] often did bit parts in pictures accompanying some actor, or simply playing the piano as part of the script. One might say that Helen and Jimmy Dietrich led a somewhat Bohemian lifestyle.

They gave really great parties, had scores of fascinating, offbeat people around them, mostly artistic, from all walks of life. I can vouch for it. One really had a good time at their parties. Everyone, it seemed, was talented and contributed to the evening's entertainment and festivities. For me, at every party occasion, it was a kind of accepted ritual for Jimmy to play some mixed musical variations while I would abandon myself totally dance-wise, improvising to each musical mood Jimmy played. It was very exhilarating to me and I reveled in it, as did Jimmy.

It was a "high" I always got at the Dietrich's parties, and better than champagne. A fascinating play could have been written about the laissez-faire lifestyle of the Dietrichs. Both of them carried on their personal amorous encounters without either one of them losing sleep over it. They were wonderful, if not quite perfect, human beings. They had one daughter, Shirley. She was somewhat mentally challenged, but a sweet and lovely girl. Shirley had one of the most exquisite natural singing voices imaginable. All that was good, true, and beautiful in her being was in her wonderful voice. It was pure, perfect pitch with velvety tones. Shirley became pregnant in her early teens and had a son. The boy married her though they soon divorced. She later had two more children, all perfectly normal and seemingly well adjusted. We lost touch over the years. Sadly, Jimmy Dietrich had a very difficult Karma to deal with. Due to acute diabetic poisoning, he had to have both legs amputated at the knee. Nevertheless, his extraordinary courage and effervescent spirit carried him through. He refused to give up and continued working until his death as a pianist in a small nightclub and restaurant in the San Fernando Valley. Helen Dietrich's life likewise ended sadly. She was stricken with paralysis and remained hospitalized until the day she died. Helen and Jimmy Dietrich enjoyed life to the fullest when it was good and they will ever remain in my memory my dear friends as the happy, gifted, vibrant people they were.

Despite the economic fallout in America, the 1930-31 movie season at Universal changed the face of movie going forever. Junior Laemmle delighted himself with a subject that was long known to him, the macabre. His sights were set to cast his favorite actor of the times, Lon Chaney, to star in a film adaptation of the classic novel, *Dracula*. Universal had purchased the rights for the novel from the estate of the late Irish author, Abraham "Bram" Stoker. Unfortunately, Lon Chaney passed away before production began. Several well-known Hollywood actors of the day were considered for the role of Count Dracula. However, the starring role eventually landed with a relatively unknown actor by the name of Bela Lugosi. And as it is said, 'the rest is history! *Dracula*, the motion picture made the Hungarian born actor synonymous with the role. Carla would now change her name from Beth and would now be known as Carla Laemmle. She was nearing her 21st birthday. Carla would be cast in this Universal Picture speaking no more than a line of dialogue in the opening of the film. Little did she know that her appearance would later become part of her legacy. In the 75-plus years since the filming of "Dracula," Carla had, in fact, ushered in the first full-sound talkie horror movie, delivering the film's first spoken lines.

As Carla Laemmle (no longer Beth) the now infamous opening coach scene with her infamous line that begins with, "Among the Rugged Peaks..." from Universal's (English version of) *Dracula*, 1931. (left to right) Dwight Frye, Carla Laemmle on Frye's lap, Nicholas Bela, Donald Murphy and Daisy Belmore. Carla was 29.

> Among the rugged peaks that frown down across the Borgo Pass, are found crumbling castles of a bygone age.

Carla remembered:

> I was taken to the wardrobe department where I was fitted with the outfit of the secretary [girl passenger] that you see in the movie. I was cast to play a rather timid, comic little secretary to a sour-faced English woman. It just so

Carla Laemmle reads to her fellow passengers in this frame enlargement from *Dracula*.

happened to be the opening coach scene in *Dracula*. I thought the eyeglasses would be a good prop. It is so amazing that after all of these years, people are treating me like some cult figure, and I love it! I am thrilled and amazed by the newfound attention that *Dracula* receives. My cousin, Carl Laemmle, Jr. produced it. There seems to be only one movie still that exists of me in *Dracula*. It is when I am falling onto the lap of the character Renfield [played by Dwight Frye] after the carriage begins to bounce around. I autograph a great many of them.

I sat across from Dwight Frye in the scene to read the dialogue and fall over his lap to give the illusion of a rough and treacherous ride. The property men were juggling the coach out of camera range. There were at least four prop men. Otherwise, it was a stationary coach, a prop with an open front.

There was another scene that I was aware of and that was the village Inn where I am standing outside the coach at the Inn alongside Dwight Frye and a couple of other actors. If you look close, you'll see me running into the Inn as the coach leaves in a long shot. I hadn't noticed, until in recent years, that memory on film.

I understand that, since 1998, I am the only surviving cast member from the movie. I receive fan mail from all over the world and I am flattered to be remembered for both *Dracula* and *The Phantom of the Opera*. It's laughable, in a way, to think that just having that one speaking part in *Dracula* that it would draw all of this attention... Be it as it may, I am happy to have been a part of both movies and I answer all fan mail.

Carl Laemmle, Jr. went on to make *Frankenstein*, the film that would make a star out of Boris Karloff—although my uncle wasn't fond of the idea of horror movies. Senior Laemmle liked Westerns. He was busy promoting Tom Mix, while Junior continued making the horror movies, all of which were moneymakers for Universal. Junior, however, is best remembered for *All Quiet on the Western Front* [1930, won the Academy Award for Best Picture and Best Director, Lewis Milstone]. He is remembered too, as the founder of the horror cycle in motion pictures, on which Universal continues to pride itself.

In the summer of 1931, Carla Laemmle appeared at the Shrine Auditorium concert in the sixth annual concert of the Los Angeles Festival Orchestra. She shared honors with cellist Mischa Gegna and soprano Teshika Sekiya. Carla gave her interpretation of Tchaikovsky's *Nutcracker Suite*. She remembers:

> Afterward, I went to a party with the Dietrich's and Jimmy introduced me to a most handsome, charismatic man. He was Russian and his name was Boris Petroff. He was a movie producer. He lived at the posh Ravenswood Apartments in Hollywood. Boris was dashing and utterly charming. I was flattered that he was so attracted to me. His pet name for me was "Carlusha." We were in a serious romantic relationship from 1931 through 1933.[16]

Los Angeles Breakfast Club Annual Meeting (1931) – In the foreground are brothers Lester and Tom H. Weber. Lester was the toastmaster and Tom the leader of the orchestra. Seated from left to right is: Orra S. Monette, Carl Laemmle, Rosabelle Laemmle Bergerman, Stanley Bergerman, Mr. and Mrs. Edward Laemmle, and Carla Laemmle.

As well as dancing, Carla was involved in many community actitivies. She and her mother remained active members of the *Daughters of the American Revolution* in the El Camino Real Chapter. Belle (mainly known after her husband's death as Mrs. Joseph Laemmle) was a Regent and the President for a term. Carla also belonged to and was President of the Juniors of the Euterpe Opera Reading Club of Los Angeles.

Carla resumed writing during this time in her life. One of her poems was submitted by her mother to *World Theology*. [17]

Since Creation's early dawn
Soul of Man progresses on
From the lower to the higher
Each a Spark of Spirit Fire

Growing both in mind and being
In the heart of All-Seeing

Boris Petroff (Producer and cinematographer at Paramount Pictures) and Carla Laemmle were in a romantic relationship from 1931-1933. (Mr. Petroff inscribed, " To Carlusha, the girl of my dreams."

    Every thought brings its reward
    Twined around a silver card

    Each new life a stepping- stone
    Where he reaps what he has sown
    Daily does he sow new seeds
    By his present thoughts and deeds

Among the Rugged Peaks

Every act returns its own
For each sin he must atone
All are chastened by this Rod
It is Karma, Law of God

Soon his span of life is done
And tho he lost, he may have won
Death claims the shell, but life goes on
His soul departs to devachan[18]
to rest awhile, far from earth's skin,
Absorb the lessons given him
Until a time when that too ends
He must return to make amends

Once more he's drawn into earth's pain,
For more experience to gain
this is the Souls Reincarnation

Evolving towards Its Destination
Divine and Glorious is this Plan
To make each being more than Man.
—Carla Laemmle, August 10, 1933

In 1934 the Opera Reading Club sponsored a benefit performance of *Romeo and Juliet*. The one-night only performance took place at the Carthay Circle Theatre in Los Angeles.[19] It starred Orion Novello as Romeo and Carla Laemmle as Juliet and the actor playing Mercutio was poet and a writer Homer Gayne. He and Carla formed a close friendship during the rehearsals. Although Homer moved to Mexico City in 1934, he and Carla continued to correspond for a while. In one of Homer's letters, dated Sunday, January 20, 1935, he composed a poem sharing his memories of Carla, who had danced in the nude one moonlit night for Homer's birthday, March 2, 1934:

> Some Moods, the Inspiration of which is Evident…
> You are…willow trees at dusk, swaying languorously under the tender caresses of the warm evening wind…. Silver sides agleam, soft leafy crown catching the last golden glow of day…You are a little girl, slim, fragile,

In 1929 Carla did a screen test photo as Juliet for Universal. In 1934 she would play Juliet opposite Orion Novello as Romeo in a benefit performance.

virginal—dancing alone—for yourself.... Seeking some unknown fulfillment of your pallid, vague, desires.

You are She, personified... Mistresses of a thousand fierce delights.... Adept in myriad sinuous phallic twining.... Atavistic memories—of matings far back in the mist of the centuries—of embraces for along, down the evolving stair—stir in your young blood and beat out wild rhythms—express themselves again-in your beautiful child-like woman's body.

You are a tiny Pierette, dancing alone in a blue spot of moonlight. The theatre is dark...The audience, once spellbound, has long since returned homeward.... Perhaps in dream you are again soon.... Perhaps calloused perspiring hands still tingle with applause, the utmost but inarticulate expression of appreciation... for something...higher, that can not be defined...a force that yearns upward.... Again, it maybe, the dreamer's dance—with you—through you—in you. You dance alone....The darkness throbs and pulsates. From the draughty wings comes a rustle....

Do other Pierettes of other days...come back... and watch...your steps...their steps, their youth—in you? Their dream...reborn, in you?.... Pierette dances alone...in a spot of blue moonlight.... Nostalgic strains of 'Blue Danube' quiver through the air. Memories of old romances, growing more sweet with the years.....Old joys...vanished youth.... Loves, almost forgotten...Bitter yet tender memories well up in the heart.... *The Blue Danube* waltzes...moonlight...perfume of kisses...*Blue Danube*....

You are a very young, very naughty girl.... You scarcely know what you are saying with your body.... It is you...but *not* you...or...is it?

Homer Gayne also wrote to Carla:

Looking Back....
"I remember dimly...as in a dream long past, faintly as the ray of a distant beacon.... One.... In flashes.... I sense although I cannot picture.... I feel but cannot know.... But of this much I am sure.... Her laughter was like tiny silver bells on the hem of a dancing girl's skirt.... Like tiny silver bells.... On the neck of a fawn.... Her laughter was like a silver coin-rolling down long white marble Stairs....

When she spoke, her voice was low and soft.... Cadenced like a fountain murmuring in the twilight....

She sang.... I almost remember... and at times, in dream I hear a strain of melody, exquisite sweeter than anything ever heard in this life...more poignant and closer to me...a melody I also have sung...long ago....

She danced...and I catch brief glimpses of her white body dancing as she used to...in the silvery sides of the trees...at sunset.... In the wildflowers that sway in the afternoon winds.... I know she danced.... I still seem, indistinctly—to see her outlined against the background of greenery...or dancing by the edge of a quiet pool, reflected in the water—that seems awed at being allowed to hold her if but for a moment.... She danced in the dusk, in the magic hour when the world again takes on a bit of the glamour of Eld.

She loved...and in flashes of ecstasy again I feel her warm mouth soft on my own...again I kiss her whiteness... once more I feel her heart throbbing...next my heart.... The nostalgic memory of her in my dream that impels on me...searching for...completion...the cell seeking its other half.... The vision that inspires to new hopes of regaining that vanished perfection.

Homer Gayne's final letter was entitled "Farewell to Maya."

I am ashamed of myself for putting this in words.... I think this will be the last effusion...that you will see.... Adios, addio, adieu, adje, desvidanya, sayonara, etc.... Hope you will be a star soon...and knock them dead. I'll always be a fond admirer and friend...and will be holding a good thought for you.... About me.... I know nothing...still don't know how long I'll be here or where I'm going.... A leaf on a stream? No...not exactly...I'm sure my Star is guiding somewhere...for some reason... unknown to be as yet...but I want to find it soon. Regards to your mother...best wishes for your Grandmother...and all the success and happiness in the world for you.
As ever...Homer.

Homer Gayne went on to sell his song lyrics, for which he was uncredited, for use in 1930s Hollywood Westerns. Carla never heard from Homer Gayne after that last letter.

Raymond Cannon, the handsome actor-turned-screenwriter from Tennessee, was hired by Universal Studios in 1934 to write scenarios. Cannon had an impressive professional background beginning with the Inceville Studio. He turned to screenwriting in the mid-1920s and worked with Selig, Goldwyn, First National Studios (later known as Warner Bros.), Fox and Columbia. By the late 1920s, he had directed three movies, *Red Wine* (1928), *Joy Street* and *Why Leave Home?* (both 1929).

Carla with her longtime friend Barbara Perry, during the filming of *Mystery of Edwin Drood* in which they both appeared.

At his time Raymond Cannon was 42 years of age and had been married and divorced. He was also the father of three children.[20]

In late 1934 director Stuart Walker (director of *Werewolf of London*,1935) was filming *The Mystery of Edwin Drood*, starring Claude Rains and David Manners. The producer was Edmund Grainger, who would go on to produce or co-produce many films including several John Wayne films such as *Wake of the Red Witch* (1948) and *Sands of Iwo Jima* (1949). The Mystery of Edwin Drood would be released in March, 1935 and was a box-office flop. Twenty-five-year-old Carla Laemmle and Barbara Perry appeared as extras in the film, and the two became good friends.

Meanwhile, producer Henry MacRae gave Raymond Cannon his first assignment at Universal. Cannon was assigned to co-write *Tailspin Tommy in the Great Air Mystery*. Directed by prolific serial and B

Western specialist Ray Taylor (*The Return of Chandu* [1934], *Flash Gordon* [1936], *The Three Mesquiteers* [1936]), the 12-episode serial was released in 1935 and starred Clark Williams (*Werewolf of London*) and Jean Rogers (*Flash Gordon*).[21]

Henry MacRae (also credited as Henry McRae), known for years at Universal for his action-adventure sequels that began in the 1920s, including *Flash Gordon*, needed a dancer and co-star to appear in a new 12-episode serial. He hired Carla Laemmle to appear in *The Adventures of Frank Merriwell*. Filmed in 1935, the serial was directed by Cliff Smith (director *Ace Drummond*, 1936 and *Secret Agent* X-9, 1937). It was released in January 1936 and starred Donald Briggs (*Captains Courageous*, 1937), John King (appeared as Dusty King in a series of B Westerns), House Peters, Jr. (*King of the Rocket Men*, 1949) and Jean Rogers. Carla was fourth billed and played a character named Carla Rogers. She appeared in every episode, and was able to perform a solo dance number that was superb!

Little did she know that her destiny was around the corner.

Carla and Barbara posing "behind the scenes" at Universal during the 1930s.

Carla Laemmla in *The Adventures of Frank Merriwell* (1935)

Act Two:
CARLA'S RAY OF LIGHT
Her Majesty the Prince
1935–1977

The year was 1935. Carla Laemmle remembers how she and Raymond Cannon met:

> It just happened. I was given an assignment to play a small part in a comedy short written by Ray, which he was to direct. Little did I know then that the course of my life would change forever through that little acting assignment and my meeting with Ray. As inexperienced as I was an actress, Ray put me to ease immediately. Right from the start we had a wonderful rapport. I had never met anyone as charismatic as Ray. From that very first day I fell under his spell.

Raymond Cannon left Universal Pictures in 1935 after one year of work.

In August of that year Carla's uncle, Carl Laemmle, wrote to Mr. Henry Duffy of the El Capitan Theatre in Hollywood:

> Dear Mr. Duffy:
> I am presuming upon your fine reputation as a stage director to introduce you to my niece, Miss Carla Laemmle. I understand that you are now starting plans for the production of the New York musical success, *Anything Goes*. Miss Laemmle is a professional dancer, and it occurred to me that you would be interested in her services for your forthcoming show. I will greatly appreciate your granting her an interview and if you find favor and give her an opportunity, I shall be grateful to you. Cordially yours, Carl Laemmle

Australian posters for the 1929 *Showboat* and the 1936 version starring Irene Dunne.

Nothing ever came of *Anything Goes* with Carla Laemmle, but she appreciated her Uncle's intentions.

The year 1935 would not be a good year for the Laemmle family. Soon after the success of *The Bride of Frankenstein*, Junior Laemmle was abandoning his fright factory for more prestigious films. His dream project was in pre-production—a remake of Universal's 1929 version of Edna Ferber's *Showboat,* which had been produced by his father.

Well into production also was a movie based on Lloyd C. Douglas' 1929 bestseller *Magnificent Obsession* starring Irene Dunne and Robert Taylor. Costs were rising because of overlapping of projects and revenues were dropping. But bad business were not the only reasons Universal was in financial trouble. It was widely known that both Laemmles, father and son, had a penchant for gambling.

The two million dollar Universal Western *Sutter's Gold* (1936) was, unfortunately, one of many reasons Universal Pictures was forced into near bankruptcy. Junior's faith in the pictures currently in production for Universal convinced his father to secure a loan. But it was too little, too late.

A Wall Street investment firm, Standard Capital Corporation, loaned $750,000 in cash to Carl Laemmle under the condition that it be repaid within 90 days. If it was not paid in 90 days, Universal would be taken over via stock purchases of $5.5 million.

Unfortunately, the loan was not paid during the allotted period; therefore Standard Capital bought 80 percent of Universal's common stock and acquired control of the company. Carl Laemmle was paid a cash settlement of $1.5 million on March 15, 1935. Ironically that was the date of the 20th anniversary of the opening of Universal.

In March 1936, Carl Laemmle resigned as president of Universal and sold his interest in the company to Standard Capital Corporation. Carl Laemmle, Jr., resigned as Vice-President and General Manager in charge of productions at Universal in April 1936. Carl Laemmle's son-in-law, Stanley Bergerman had previously resigned from his post at Universal in 1935.

It was rumored Carl Laemmle might have to sell Universal Studio. Surprisingly, Laemmle's main concern during this time was resuming the Jewish Relief War Effort. Stanley Bergerman joined forces with his father-in-law and they signed numerous affidavits that brought German-born Jews (relatives and friends), who were fleeing the horrors in Europe, to America. "Carl Laemmle was motivated from his heart," said Stanley Bergerman in 1997.

> This all came from an inner sincerity of the man. His impulses were noble, "do it." He helped because he had a great sense of appreciation of his own prosperity and his own opportunities. And there was no conscience effort on his part to be really identified by religion. He was an American. He was Jewish by faith, by religious faith, but he wanted to be identified as an American first; a philanthropist, a man of unusual effort to benefit humanity, in appreciation for what humanity may have done for him. He signed, as I was told, about 250 such guarantees for souls who he's led out of the Hitler ovens, brought out of the ovens. The State Department thought that he had perhaps exhausted his financial words and his guarantees, so he went to friends, including me. And I followed.

Both *Magnificent Obsession* and *Showboat* were released in 1936 after Standard Capital took control of Universal. Respectively, directors John Stahl and James Whale, who were originally hired by Laemmle, had completed their movies. The credits for Showboat read "Produced by Carl Laemmle, Jr."

By 1937 Raymond Cannon had become a public relations director for the newly developed China City, a unique and colorful new Chinatown. His job was to publicize and stage various kinds of theatrical events. Carla participated in many of them, including the traditional Chinese Moon Festival where she performed

Ray Cannon directed *Swing It Sailor!* in 1937.

a Chinese dance on a large platform erected in the center of the main China City Square. These events got a lot of publicity and drew crowds of people to China City. Carla said, "It was great to be part of it. It was something neither I nor Ray would ever regret."

Under Universal's new management, Charles Rogers and J. Cheever Cowdin, many changes occurred. The Joseph Laemmle family were graciously given until April 1937 to relocate. Those affected by the change were Carla, her mother, Carrie Belle Laemmle, and Carla's grandmother, Emogene Loomis Norton. This was not an easy transition because of Emma Norton's advanced age.

During the first year of their relationship, Carla had learned of Ray's deep interest in the Eastern philosophies. In Ray's past he had been to China and had spent several months in a Buddhist monastery. Carla remembers:

> I too had long been attracted to the Eastern philosophy. We had a common bond and our relationship blossomed. I learned also, that while Ray was in China he had become fascinated with the Chinese theatre. Within a few weeks after our first meeting, he wrote an utterly enchanting play for me, *Her Majesty the Prince*. I played the part of a Princess, Quan Mui Mai on and off stage! It was a fulfilling and happy time in my life. It was produced at the Music Box Theatre in Hollywood and opened May

10, 1936. The play had a three-week run with excellent reviews. Arthur Kay wrote the lovely musical score. When I met him, Ray was living with a Chinese family. He had many friends within the Chinese community. One friend that we made during the play was one of the three musicians hired. He was the violinist. His name was Lawrence Sommers. Lawrence was a friend to Jimmy and Helen Dietrich. Lawrence was a gifted and brilliant violinist. His wife, Anne was very charming. They all became close friends to Ray and myself.

Soon after *Her Majesty the Prince* closed, Ray Cannon left California for Mexico to help in the production of a movie there. He was gone for six weeks, leaving Carla behind. During this time, Ray and Carla began a written correspondence. Over the next six decades, Carla had saved both sets of love letters between she and Ray Cannon. When she released these letters to this writer, a note attached read:

> These love letters from Ray were written in 1936 during the months of July and August when he was working on a film in Mexico with Miguel Torres.[1] The originals of the letters will be a part of the Carla Laemmle Collection at the Los Angeles Natural History Museum. I think I can truly say they are my most cherished possession. They are so beautifully moving to me, and reflect the inner beauty of Ray's soul. I was so blessed to have had the love of this man in my life. I look forward to the point in time—in the eternity of things when we will be together again. Our beings will surely be drawn to one another. We have other wonderful destinies to fulfill. Carla.

Ray left Los Angeles by train Tuesday morning, July 28, 1936. The following letters were chosen amongst over 300 pages of letters between Carla and Ray. They created the foundation from which their relationship was based. Ray's first letter to Carla was while he traveled by train.

> Darling—
> This train is so rough I am not sure you can read any of this. Flash——Saw a cloudburst near Yuma. Passed near

the great All-American Canal under construction. Only three old men in my car—some dumb school teachers in tow in car ahead, then the rabble so to work on The Mongolian Emperor. Your letter is so lovely—lovely like you, yourself. I shall think of you every night at 7 and 11—I'm not sure which —you intended. I can't make it out. I will try to get contact at those hours—Pacific time. Already I miss you. I wonder how I will go to sleep? I know I will work until morning—no, I can't do that. I must get up at 8am in El Paso and see the Mexican Counsel. Anyway I can work till three. We passed the rainstorm just in time to see a glorious sunset. I wonder if you are seeing one? Look for them and I will send a message by the setting sun to you. You will see in the golden reflections of the setting suns rays—the warmth of the love of my heart for you. Everyday I shall send this message. I have written this without thinking or planning—just my thoughts. The next one I will try to do better, ok? Can't remember how to spell Lemmele? Lemela? Llemmla? P.S. I saw a lot of swell fishing tackle at one of the stock shops I passed —Yours, Ray.

Dearest Ray,
Received your letter this morning with great joy. Even you forgot how to spell Laemmle"—ha ha—-! Would Mrs. R. Cannon be any easier? Yes dear I meant seven o'clock but I don't think it's a very good hour—besides there's a difference of several hours isn't there? Shall we make it 11 here? What time would it be then for you—too late I fear. I am thinking of you all the time anyway, so it really doesn't matter to me which hour we choose. About my days activities—I spent the day with Eve, Willon's wife and had dinner there and then we all went to the [Hollywood] Bowl. I stopped by for Mama—the show wasn't so good. They had a ballet put on by a teacher at S.C. University and it was terrible as you can imagine.

Willon's wife is crazy about fishing too and they have some grand tackle so perhaps she and I will go one day next week. She is a rather nice girl after you know her, though I didn't like her at first. Darling, I came across a new thought in [the book] *The Hill of Dreams* that struck me as something to ponder over. I will quote from the book, "The fancy that sensations are symbols and not realities hovered in his mind and led him to speculate as to whether they could not actually be transmitted one into the another. It was possible a whole continent of knowledge had been undiscovered."

He could imagine a man who was able to line in one sense while he pleased to whom, for example, every impression of touch, taste, hearing, or seeing should be translated into odor; who at the desired kiss should be ravished with the scent of dark violets, to whom music should be the perfume of a rose- garden at dawn.' Isn't that an unusual that? I will quote others later.

Well, you arrive in Mexico tomorrow, finally. You will have a letter awaiting you. I am enjoying writing to you. It takes the place of talking somehow, in a small way. We are going to look for a house tomorrow. I am rehearsing again also—Yes sweetheart—I shall regard each sunset as a special love offering for me. That's a beautiful "that!" And each breeze that caresses you will carry my love to you. Goodnight darling—-Carla.

Ray dearest,
Only 20 hours have passed since you left yesterday, yet it seems an interminably long time, and to think you haven't even arrived—this is terrible darling.

I practiced or rather rehearsed this afternoon quite strenuously—had to break in my new toe shoes. I saw Mr. Herscher later and he has made a new arrangement of my song—it's greatly improved.

Saw Barbara Barondess [later Mrs Douglas MacLean] while getting a dish of ice cream.

She wanted to know if anything was going to be done with the play.

Darling, you remember I told you one morning about a crazy woman who came to the house and asked for me and left that strange note with the heading "Scientific Order of the Holy Bell'?

Well, Mama received just as crazy a letter, which I will enclose—tell me what you make of it and return it to me.

I am sitting here in the dining room munching on popcorn—it's very good too—I made it myself!

I am having lunch with Willon Field's wife tomorrow. They live over in Burbank now.

He is working at Warner's First National. Don't worry I shan't go out with him. Well sweet —I guess I'll go to bed—I hope you're having a pleasant journey—wish I were along. All my love to you, my dear—for always, Carla.

My Precious One,

Two letters came today. They are treasures—like nectar to the heart. Do send more often and long. I need them so much. I have never felt such an urge as the one I feel now.

I am almost overwhelmed by a mad desire to run back to you tonight—a little cracked, yes? I shall have to work even harder to keep my balance. Every time there is a moment's pause, my thoughts jump quickly to you and when I see beautiful things I talk to you about them. It seems as though you can hear me.

I noticed you found my message in the sunset even before I wrote to you about them.

Yes, the message told of my love.

I live with the Mr. and Mrs. Torres in the swankiest apt in town. My room is lovely. We have a roof garden. I work there among the flowers. I take long walks for exercise through a lovely park. I see many Indians make love there. Most everything delivered is carried by Indians. A strap across the forehead holds a package in place on the back.

Yesterday, I saw the Cafe San Angles and had tea there. This is the most charming spot yet. It was an old monastery, but with a refined rusticity. Spanish tiled fountains almost 400 years old—gardens—old orchards—vines covering a jungle-like atmosphere with beds of very fragrant flowers. Gardenias and orchids and the life! A glorious patio, but all the houses here have beautiful patios.

I just heard the policeman's whistle. They go around all night blowing every hour. There, I heard another one answer him. The tone is very pleasant. It is not shrill like our police whistle—it has a harmonious two-note tone. More love than I can tell my sweet.

Good night—I kiss you, Ray.

My Princess,
You can't realize how much your letters mean to me. I didn't know until today, for two days I haven't received one and I am almost dying of loneliness. If the next mail doesn't bring one I will be lost.

With the sunset I sent you my promise of eternal devotion. Not a pretend appearance of gallantry or of fleeting dalliance in amorousness, but a vital constant adoration that for "all time to come, warm the heart and calm the turbulence of mental tempests ever trying to create cheerfulness as we wander down that long lane of life, living the enchanting good years.

I am writing this in the roof garden. The sun is sitting beneath rain-laden clouds lasting its rays through the mountain mists. From this snow-capped volcano a rainbow curves to the tropical valley below. A warm balmy breeze blows thru this scented garden. Yet all this beauty I would quickly trade for one breath of woodland and white clover.

Today, I walked again in Chapultepec gardens. I saw more Aztec ruins and garden spots you were with me—I felt the touch of your warm hand—I was enthralled with each new beauty because of your presence.

At times I was sure I was living something of the past over again and that we did stroll among those same ancient trees not so many lives ago. It seemed so familiar. I seemed to remember each curve of the little lakeletts. Perhaps you were an Aztec princess and I, some stray mountain swain who dared climb the walls of your exalted fathers castle gardens and woo one of the royal house even though death be the penalty. I felt such an intensity as I strolled beneath those long mosses covered caressing arms of trees that stood there then.

Writing this letter relieves my loneliness yet I am afraid to read it over for fear, I will seem slightly unbalanced. Always——I love you, Ray.

My darling,
Received two letters from you today. I don't see why they always have to come all at once. It seems so long before more get here. So I just read the others over and over.

It must be very beautiful from your descriptions and I should have to go there some day. But darling, you haven't mentioned the picture [movie] yet—all I gathered from your letters was that you were busy seeing Mexico. I do want to know how the picture is coming along. Please tell me about it dear. You won't have to stay longer than five weeks will you? It will just be two weeks ago tomorrow that you left. Oh, I'm so lonesome for you, Ray.

You said I should write more often—I like that! When I've written every single day! I can't help it if the postal service is slow.

I got a book of plays from the library today and *The Yellow Jacket* is one of them. I have been reading it today. It is nothing to compare with "our" play—we'll show them— won't we?

Mama and I went to the show tonight—saw *Sutter's Gold* and *Till we Meet Again*. Both were good pictures. I was surprised at "Sutter's Gold" for I had heard it wasn't so good.

Darling, whenever I feel blue or discouraged I think of what you wrote in one of your letters, that I must be ready 365 days from now and it acts like a tonic for me mentally. Maybe dearest, I am depending on you too much, but I don't feel like tackling anything without you and your advice—That's bad.

Sweetheart, I guess I have the same urge as you had because I should like you to come back tonight. My arms are aching to hold you and my lips seek yours— but you're so far away. Please hurry back. I'm as crazy as you are, I guess.

I will say goodnight now, as I am getting sleepy. All my love—Carla.... P.S. I have kissed this little flower and with it goes my heart.

Dear One,
I have been rushed so rapidly I have had no time to write. Miguel and Mrs. are showing me the town and I have seen so many interesting things. It would require a volume to explain and picture half the beauty.

I shall never go on a trip again without you. Every little thing I see causes pain of agony because you are not with me. I see so many things that I know would thrill you, so much! Chapultepec gardens and castle where some of the trees were planted before Cortez came with the Spanish Conquers —planted by Montezuma, the Indian's Emperor, with all the interior is truly a palace of grandeur. The varied art is overwhelming. Murals, paintings, drapes—furnishings are real art. One cannot help being stirred by ambition—to build castles and gardens of glamour.

The wealth of beauty of most every street of this town is enough to inspire the poets of the world. There is not an alley without it's ancient building. The charm of these mosses covered antiquated houses are really enchanting. Miguel thinks I'm a bit batty when I stop and gaze so long at them. I don't believe Paris, Venice or any other European city can compare with this one, the exquisite traditional beauty.

All the loveliness I see I store away for us. My one—Ray.

My Charming One,
Your letters get better and better and I will have to insist on you writing things all the time. Your choice of words, your phrasing and the thoughts clearly defined. It would be funny if you became a writer of note—-then I suppose I would have to become a dancer.—Ha Ha!

Anyway, your method of expressing your thoughts with the pen will give you a lovely manner of speech. Is it not therefore a great benefit?

I'll be home two or three days after you get this letter. We have one more day to shoot and I feel sure we will have Saturday night.

I was never so restless—I am so anxious to get back to you and get to work on important things. The trip here has been a great benefit to me in many ways but I feel that I, or we will do really good ones. So be ready for a lot of activity...

...Don't quit writing to me until I send you an airmail letter telling you just the day I'm leaving. It looks like Tuesday or Wednesday now and I don't think it will be later... I am sure I would soon be close to you and feel the wine-like caresses of your lips, the penetrating warmth of your breath on me—the reflection of divine passion in your eyes and to enter with you into that oblivious of ecstasy and the million other things that are parts of the good life. My love, Ray.

My beloved,
Another letter came late yesterday afternoon—they are all so precious to me. After rehearsal last night I went to see *The Mystery of Verdun*, a Federal Theatre project.

Helen gave me a pass for it. She had seen it before and told me that Orion [Novello] was in it and that he was excellent. So, I wanted to see it naturally. I got there a little late but saw enough to know what it was about. It is propaganda against war and shows what would happen if all the dead soldiers were resurrected and returned to their homes. It is gruesome and lacks contrast and would never be a success here. Well, to get back to Orion. He was one of the dead soldiers and had a fair part, but I didn't think he showed any great exhibition of acting. He was supposed to speak in a slow dead voice that is comparatively easy for most any amateur. I went backstage later to see him and did he give me the cold shoulder! He said there was nothing more for us to say to one another and was very rude and insulting.

I talked later with Pat Reynolds who is also in the play and told her what he said and she believes as I do that his mind is effected. I actually believe he's insane. She said he acts as strangely—tells the director he can't act unless everything is quiet around him and he has to hear music to be able to express his soul, etc. He is going with one of the girls in the group and has forbidden her to speak to any man in the theatre. He's going to marry her it seems. So I shall never go near him again. The things he left at my house I'll throw away. I wouldn't lower myself to even speak with him.[2]

More and more I appreciate your sincere and unselfish love for me—and I shall never do anything to spoil it—a love like ours comes only once in a lifetime. Darling, our affairs are reaching a crisis—my Uncle wants Mama to sign over the trust deed and our lawyer advises her not to. It is all terribly involved and I don't know how it will turn out. If I only had a steady income it would make matters easier, but if the $45.00 should stop, as it undoubtedly would—where would we be? I don't know what Mama should do. I think it is very unfair and greedy of Carl L. to press it so, don't you? He has only a few million dollars, poor man! Will close now, dearest, with all my love—for Always—Carla.

My sweet,

I have come to the conclusion that there is no life without you. Everything I see is important only because of you. I find myself exerting much care in observation of strange little things so that may tell you abou them—funny things—artistic buildings—colorful gardens, odd people and their habits. Everything I collect for you. It makes life much fuller. My work most of all is a hundred times more interesting because of you. Yet I know all these things are a great benefit to me. Do you feel good when you know you are so much inspiration to me?

    No doubt it is this urge that makes great men do things—the wanting to make someone very proud of them, then to be praised, comforted and loved by that one. For me this would be the great reward—add to this the acclaim of intelligent peoples and a splendid life is envisioned.

    I know you are quite concerned at present with the problems of security —give this little thought, but rather let it set as stimulant to accomplish the quicker. All the eagerness you can pile up will not be too much—but don't let it disturb the serenity of your mind. Your poise under all conditions are necessary to the good of your health and beauty. Permit no act of man to rob you of your constructive thoughts and all earthly evil must quickly pass focus of your vision, but its impression be recorded on the portion of the mind most needed for observing beauty. And the power of perception become dimmed and valueless...

    ...The prospects of our future seems brighter now than ever, and accomplishing them seems easy...

    I am all confused about—the trust deed business. A trust deed can be foreclosed 30 days after it becomes due while it requires at least a year to take over a piece of property by foreclosure of a mortgage. I think it would be well for your mother to write to Uncle and explain her bewilderment at his sudden change of heart telling him that she wants his advise. If your mother does sign insist that the paper be for a long period of time—five or 10 years—if possible.

However things go you and I will do our stuff soon and show a lot of people. I love you all my darling. Ray.

Friday afternoon—August 28th
My darling,

Well, here I am like I promised this morning—getting today's letter in on time. I was in such a rush this morning when I wrote, so many people came in that I was delayed in writing, but I got it off alright before my lesson.

First of all, this morning, early, before I was up, that crazy lady came over again. This time she wanted Mama to allow her to use our mailbox for letters coming to her. She also told Mama that Carl Laemmle Junior was going to be the Savoir of the World, that it was proven or rather revealed to her by the stars, planets and what have you! She said that she had already had a long talk with Laemmle Sr. And that he would do anything he could to help her. I don't believe a word of that or part of it either. She also wanted Mama to help her get in touch with Junior. Did you ever hear anything so insane? I only heard part of the conversation—I was listening from the bedroom. Then shortly after I had gotten up and had breakfast, Curley Robinson[3] came. He couldn't make it last night. He said that he thought it would be better instead of writing Thalberg, to go back and talk with Stanley Bergerman as he knows Irving very well. Have Stanley talk to him about me. Well it may be ok but I don't think I shall do anything until you come back and I know what is going to happen.

By the way, before I forget, we saw Mr. Feiler again this afternoon and he had a talk with Mr. Raesel and he said that the $45.00 would continue again—without obligation—which is swell. We hadn't received it for two weeks now. Also Mr. Feiler had an offer for the acre property in Huntington Park so it would be fine if she could sell it now.

Well, to get back—-while Curley was still here, who should come over but Baxter Gamble. He is still working on *Flying Hands*, that deaf mute picture and expects to start shooting in three weeks. Well, he asked me if I would play the lead in it. Imagine? I'd have to learn sign language in three weeks! Not that I couldn't or wouldn't if I thought the picture would mean anything. After all, he is directing it and acting in it and is only costing $4500.00 to make. I am afraid of it. It would be worse than *The Adventures of Frank Merriwell*. Well, I told him that I expected to go on with the Chinese play as soon as you return from Mexico and that I wouldn't have time. He asked me anyway to come down Sunday and watch the rehearsals, so I may drop by—it would be interesting to see deaf mutes rehearse, once.

Your letter this morning was lovely—tonight I shall try to remember when we were there in Xochimilco. But what happened after you sang so beautifully to me? Didn't I respond to your plea of love? How wonderful it would be if we could go back, in ages past and trace our lives in each succeeding incarnation up to the present one. Wouldn't it make a most fascinating story?

Even our conversations that we have had in this life are not ordinary and would make a story themselves. As I think of them now, I actually thrill as some of the things you spoke about come back to me. We spent so many strange and delightful moments didn't we?

You taught me so much—with all the patience and understanding of a God—and you found something in me that no one else had ever seen. You tenderly and carefully nurtured it until it is now blossoming and growing so that other people see it. And with it all has come a peace of mind and heart that only comes by pure thoughts and loving the good life. I never want any other kind. I love you always, Your Princess.

Friday August 28 [1936] ...
Darling,

One month ago today I left Hollywood and you. It seems a year. After this when I go away, you go with me or I don't go.

Tomorrow night I catch the train to come to you—and it is you I want to come to, not Hollywood. Yet I know it will be only our starting place—because we are going places and soon.

I hope you are feeling fit when I get there because if you feel as I do we are going to have some very interesting times. And I don't mean just fishing alone. (I just noticed that my face etc. is burning.) I will be in a very exaltable mood if my feelings continue to increase. I am about the most healthy person you have ever known. I have had a few sunbaths and am quite brown. I have lost two inches around the waist, the result of walking—and an accumulation of energy that is almost overwhelming. Something must be done about it when I get there...

I have got a new angle on {The] *Mongolian* [Emperor] and I know you will burst with excitement when I tell you all about it.... I kiss you with all of me, my love. And send a wish that you feel the warmth of the caress. I send also my spirit to comfort you till I arrive. May all your thoughts be bathed in the mist of the rainbow of loveliness—Ray.

Ray returned to Los Angeles by the *Sunset Limited* train that arrived at the South Pacific Station in Los Angeles on Wednesday, September 2, 1936, one day after his 44th birthday.

Consequently, after less than a year of employment at MGM, a dissatisfied Carl Laemmle, Jr. bought his contract back from MGM and turned his back on movie production. He would never work in movies again.

It was a shock to the Hollywood elite when on Monday morning, September 14, 1936 Irving Grant Thalberg, passed away at the age of 36. Chairmanship of the Motion Picture Producers' Association, created by Mr. Thalberg only eight months earlier, was soon voted to Darryl

Zanuck. At the funeral, Rabbi Edgar F. Magnin conducted the service. *Variety*, reported (September 23, 1936; Page 3):

> Few persons saw the arrival of the funeral cortege in Forest Lawn. Even representatives of the press kept at a distance and there were no cameras. The feeling of a great loss was everywhere felt and the reverent spirit was in great contrast to other funerals.

Both Senior and Junior Laemmle were away in Europe at the time of Mr. Thalberg's death. Rosabelle Laemmle Bergerman remained at home in Beverly Hills. Irving Thalberg was survived by his wife, famed actress Norma Shearer, and their two children, Irving Thalberg, Jr. and Katherine. Carla remembered Mr. Thalberg as "a gifted and highly intelligent producer." She said that her Uncle Carl must have seen something of himself in young Irving Thalberg when he first hired him at Universal. Carla said:

> I would see Irving Thalberg at many of the social gatherings. He was a good looking and kind-hearted person, much like his sister Sylvia was.

In January 1937, Carla, her mother, and her grandmother, said goodbye to Universal City after 16 years of residence. Carla found a house to rent in Hollywood on Mariposa Street while Ray was away. Carla remembers:

> In fact it was in 1937. Four months after we made the bittersweet move from Universal to Mariposa Street my grandmother, Emogene Isabella Loomis Norton, passed away at home [May 27, 1937] at the age of 91.

Many loved Emma Norton including Carl Laemmle. When he learned of Emma's death, he graciously arranged her funeral. She is interred at Forest Lawn Cemetery in Glendale, California. Emma Norton, experienced a great many changes during her long life and one of the things she was most grateful for was seeing her daughter and granddaughter grow to womanhood as law-abiding, voting citizens.

Carla explains why she and Ray never married:

> Well, in the early days the timing wasn't right for it. Ray didn't have a steady job, money was scarce, and my mother needed me. Later, marriage was not a priority. The truth is, I felt that Ray and I were united by a far more enduring bond that has brought us together again and again, life after life, over the centuries, and will continue to do so in the eternity of things. Ray likewise believed in reincarnation and that we had shared many lifetimes together.

Labor unrest in Hollywood began in 1936 with the IATSE (International Association of Theatrical Stage Employees). By 1937 the Supreme Court had upheld the National Labor Relations Act (also known as the Wagner Act of 1935) guaranteeing the right of employees to form unions and bargain collectively.

Unions launched campaigns in Hollywood for a closed shop, which required all workers to join a union. The stronghold of unionism in Hollywood was and still is S.A.G. (Screen Actors' Guild).[4] The original members of the Screen Actors' Guild established themselves in 1933.[5] In that same year, studios, pleading poverty, cut in half the salaries of every actor in Hollywood saying the cut would avert tremendous layoffs. When the cut was accomplished, studios proceeded to effect drastic layoffs anyway.[6]

Carl Laemmle made his last trip to Europe in the summer of 1938. Accompanied by his son they visited Zurich, Switzerland. Because of the political climate, Mr. Laemmle could not enter his hometown of Laupheim, Germany. He had made his last trip there in 1933. While Carl was in Zurich he sent a postcard, dated August 15, 1938, to Belle Laemmle and Carla that simply read, "Still thinking of you. Love, Carl Laemmle."

Carl had moved his remaining brother Siegfried and his wife Betty from Munich to America before the end of 1938.

Hollywood faced many changes during the 1930s. Tinseltown scandals increased the perception of Hollywood as a den of vice and decadence. Trying to avoid government regulation, the studios agreed to form the Legion of Decency to oversee the content of movies. A crackdown headed by the former Chairman of the Republican Party Will Hays began in earnest in July 1934.

But Washington D.C. wasn't done with Hollywood. In 1938 the House Un-American Activities Committee (known as HUAC) was formed by Congress. James B. Matthews, a former Communist told the committee that James Cagney, Bette Davis, Clark Gable, Miriam Hopkins and Shirley Temple were unwittingly serving communist interests. Careers and lives were ruined by the witch hunter who saw red everywhere. If it wasn't so sickening and depressing it would be laughable. And for the record, no one in the Laemmle family was a communist sympathizer.

The changing world political climate was also affecting Hollywood and movies. The year 1938 was the prelude to a World War that lasted six years. The world had not recovered from WWI when China invaded Japan on Wednesday, July 7, 1937, only six years since they previously invaded in 1931. Both invasions hindered Chinese trade to the United Kingdom of Great Britain and Northern Ireland. March 12, 1938 Adolf Hitler marched into Austria proclaiming a political and geographical union of Germany and Austria. September 1, 1939 Germany invaded Poland and three days later most of the world was once again at war.

Carl Laemmle was enjoying his retirement, especially spending more time with his two grandchildren Carol Bergerman and Stanley Bergerman, Jr. His peaceful existence would come to a halt on the evening of November 9, 1938. It was on that night that Hitler launched an attack on Jews living in Germany and the lands it had invaded. That horrific evening became known as Kristallnacht or The Night of Broken Glass. Laupheim's only Synagogue, temple of the Laemmle family, was set on fire that night. The structure burned for two days.

Carl Laemmle, the tough businessman, was at heart a sentimentalist and took the reports coming out of Germany very hard. He felt deeply for his native town of Laupheim, Germany. Laemmle, too old to pick up a weapon against the Nazis, helped in the only way he knew how—by aiding European women, children and men escape the terror of Hitler and immigrate to America. Laemmle did this over 300 times.

Although not in the same straits as the European Jews, the plight of the people of the Chinese community of Los Angeles were just as important to Raymond Cannon as the people of Germany were to Carl Laemmle.

A small group of Old China enthusiasts began meeting at the Golden Dragon Cafe in the late months of 1938. Hoping to promote the culture and arts of China, they realized how varied and extensive the activity of their contemplated organization would be.

It is impossible to complete the roster of persons who took part in the early informal meetings that lead to the final organization of the Chinese Culture Society. However, among the newspaper clippings of November 11, 1938 appears this account of one of the largest Golden Dragon affairs under the auspices of Mrs. Joseph Laemmle.

> More than 100 men and women this week inaugurated the first of a series of Wednesday evening dinners and tours of China City, under the auspices of Mrs. Joseph Laemmle.
>
> One of the very first to take a natural interest in the contemplated Society was Mr. Ray Cannon, one time resident in China. On diplomatic missions Mr. Cannon had acquired both a taste and knowledge of the Chinese way of life, their arts, and theatre. Here he was at home being long associated with the theatre arts and among the earliest of motion picture directors in Hollywood. Mr. Cannon was among those present at the steering committee meeting that took place in late December 1938.

The Friday morning January 6, 1939 *Los Angeles Times* reported:

> New Chinese Culture Club Formed
>
> Wednesday evening, January 4, 1939 at a dinner at the Junk Cafe in China City, the new Chinese Cultural Society was permanently organized. Officers named were, Raymond Cannon, executive secretary, and Mrs. Joseph Laemmle, Director. Mr. Wing Foo [Chinese baritone] was named program chairman. Mrs. Franklin B. MacCarthy was named Chairman of the Ways and Means Committee assisted by Carla Laemmle.[7]

During their first six years, countless committee meetings were held at the home of Mrs. Joseph Laemmle. Carla Laemmle and Ray Cannon were among the executive committee that included Francis E. Baxter, Mabelle James, Elizabeth Howard Hyde, Judge L.R. Wharton and Mrs. Wharton, Mrs. Lawrence Sommers, Jack Landor, Miss Florence W. Howell, David Chow, Mrs. Frances E. Payne, Mrs. Cima Pollia, Harvey Parker and Naomi Reynolds.

Many friends of Carla Laemmle were pressed into service. Among the outstanding speakers were Manly P. Hall (Canadian mystic and author of *The Secret Teachings of All Ages*, 1928) and Hollywood actor Keye Luke (number one son in the 1930s Charlie Chan films and Kato in 1940 *The Green Hornet*), whose lecture on Chinese Art became preserved in the Society's history.

The *Genesis of the History of the Chinese Culture Society*, reads:

> They envisioned the pleasures of examining together the broad gamut of life encompassed by the China that finally passed in the revolution of 1911. This was the China which long centuries was the antithesis of the dynamic country which our day is so rapidly absorbing the culture of the West. It was the China in which men spent whole lifetimes working at the creation of one art piece, the completion of which was often passed on to their sons. It was the long, long China of the leisurely life, when every public man of the empire took time out to steep himself in the poetry, the art and the philosophical classics of the great masters and the national eras preceding his own. And it was the China when every official of consequence was deemed an incomplete citizen unless he was able to contribute something original to the national cultural treasure in the form of poetry.

Friday September 1, 1939 was Ray Cannon's 47th birthday, the day the Germans invaded Poland. Carla had resumed working in motion pictures in 1938 by auditioning for MGM producer Bernard H. Hyman (producer of *Camille* and *San Francisco*, both 1936) and ballet choreographer, Albertina Rasch (with whom she had worked with previously in 1929 at MGM). Carla was a Strauss enthusiast and her dancing expertise won her a part in Hyman's production of *The Great*

Carla Laemmle dances in *On Your Toes* (Warner Bros., 1939).

Waltz, starring Luise Rainer and Fernand Gravey (credited as Gravet) as Johann Strauss. Following *The Great Waltz,* Carla auditioned at Warner Bros. for a forthcoming musical. Director Ray Enright, who began in the business gag writing for Mack Sennett, hired famed ballet choreographer

Carla (center) with the ballet ensemble practice in *On Your Toes*.

George Balanchine to audition dancers for the film. Carla auditioned for Mr. Balanchine and was hired as a dancer for the 1939 movie *On Your Toes*, although she was uncredited in the film. The film was from the play by George Abbott, and had been performed on Broadway 315 times during the 1936-37 season. The motion picture version of *On Your Toes* was really a vehicle for Balanchine's wife, ballerina Vera Zorina and included the famous ballet "Slaughter on Tenth Avenue." The ballet was later reprised by Gene Kelly and Vera-Ellen. Carla is proud to have worked with one of the most prominent and celebrated choreographers of the 20th century.

Carla, now 29, was at an advantage in Hollywood—she had been a member of Actor's Equity since 1927. No longer under contract to any studio, she was able to seek employment anywhere. Despite the tough economic times in Tinseltown, Carla auditioned for many jobs. Unwilling to trade on the Laemmle name, Carla's first cousin Rosabelle Laemmle suggested Carla change her name to Carol Lenard and join the American Guild of Variety Artists. For the next 14 years Carla was known professionally as Carol Lenard.

On a Sunday morning at 11:30 a.m., Carl Laemmle, passed away at his Beverly Hills home. At his side were Carl, Jr., daughter Rosabelle

Carl Laemmle (1939 photo) 1867-1939.

Bergerman, son-in-law Stanley Bergerman and three physicians; Dr. Hawkins, Dr. Stanley Immerman and Dr. Morris Nathanson. Laemmle, Sr. was 72. His death, on September 24, 1939, was international news and received lengthy coverage in the *Los Angeles Times*, the *New York Times* and *Daily Variety*.

Carla and her mother Belle were among the mourners at the Wilshire Boulevard Temple the following day where the body of Laemmle lay in state. The services were officiated by Rabbi Edgar F. Magnin, who was considered the dean of American Rabbis.[8] At 12:30 p.m. all of the Hollywood studios suspended work to pay a silent tribute to the producer. The same rare tribute had occurred for Irving Thalberg three years previously.

Rabbi Magnin delivered the eulogy for a death that was mourned all over the world:

> The poor boy who came over from Germany made America richer in many ways. He was a pioneer in one of the greatest industries and arts in the world, one which reaches the lives and hearts and souls of countless millions of people, and he used his office for the welfare and improvement of his fellow men. Many of the pictures he made were classics of the screen. They brought education, enlightenment and a spiritual life to those who saw them.
>
> Born in Europe, Laemmle never forgot his birthplace, but he was an American, not a European. He had one allegiance and one loyalty to the country of his adoption, and there were more like him in America today, there would be less of alienisms and distorted European propaganda. Famous stars and producers, the simple workingmen, bankers and beggars, industrial potentates and those who work with their hands, all bow their heads in grief.

Pallbearers included Jack Ross, who had been Laemmle's personal secretary, Ben Strauss, a May Company executive and friend of the family, David Tannenbaum, Laemmle's personal attorney, producer Sam Von Ronkle and Herman Einstein, who was a refugee Laemmle had helped immigrate from his native Laupheim, Dr. Leland Hawkins, Laemmle's personal physician, and friends of the family Sam Behrendt and Fred S. Meyer. His body was placed in a vault at the Home of Peace Cemetery pending the decision of the family on interment.

Carl Laemmle was survived by his son Carl, Jr., daughter Rosabelle Bergerman, son-in-law Stanley Bergerman, brothers, Louis and Siegfried, sister-in-law Anna Stern Fleckles and his two grandchildren Carol, age 9, and Stanley Bergerman, Jr., age 7. In addition, Mr. Laemmle was also survived by a number of cousins, nephews and nieces, including of course, Carla Laemmle. Ogden Nash, one of America's best-known humorist once wrote that "Uncle Carl Laemmle has a large faemmle."

Carla Laemmle remembers her Uncle Carl Laemmle this way:

> My earliest memory of my uncle, Carl Laemmle, was of his beaming, sunny smile. When he smiled, his eyes and whole face lit up. It was so delightfully disarming that you were instantly won over. In fact, his smile became somewhat of a trademark....the Laemmle smile. I have always had the highest admiration and affection for my uncle. I only regret that I never had the opportunity to express my feelings during his lifetime. He was a truly remarkable man in so many ways. As a pioneer in the early days of the developing film industry, his contributions and achievements were unique. He was very generous, extremely generous to his friends and to people. He was a square shooter. He was so honest in his dealings, he was a stickler at it. Everything he said, any promises he ever made, he kept. He didn't need a contract because his word was his bond. He was a man of honor and integrity, all the way. He was always positive. He never gave up. His motto became, "It Can Be Done." And he stuck to it.
>
> But it is only in these latter years that I have come to learn more about my uncle's personal activities and to appreciate what a great humanitarian he was. If he could see Universal today, he would be dumbfounded with its growth and civilization. The hill behind Universal was just a hill. Now there is a hotel sitting there. But, I feel that his "legacy is certainly with his heartfelt commitment to the German refugees and all the efforts that he did in giving them affidavits, hundreds of them. And I believe that Carl Laemmle left this world a lot better place for having been in it. He was special in every way. He was

just a wonderful human being. He looked like a little old man, but in achievements he was a giant. He really liked people and cared about them. He also cared about the people who worked for him and he would inquire about them. He knew their families. In fact, whenever he traveled he got to know the people and he was interested in them. He was always concerned about their welfare. And if they needed his help, he would give it. He was gracious and willing.

The City of Laupheim has recently converted a former 15th Century medieval castle into a museum dedicated to the common history of Jewish and non-Jewish people who lived together there for over two centuries. Three rooms in the Museum have been commemorated to Carl Laemmle. There is also a school named after my uncle in Laupheim. Carl, himself, attended the predecessor of the school from 1878 to 1880. The birthplace of the Carl Laemmle family, of course, is Laupheim, Germany.[9] I had the great pleasure of visiting Laupheim, the school and the Museum, although the Museum was not yet completed. I made three trips in 1997, 1998 and again in 1999. As a guest of Dr. Bayer and his family, I received a most royal welcome each time from the Mayor, the Press and the people of Laupheim. The Museum had it's official opening May 15, 2003.

The following tribute was written by Carla Laemmle for this book:

TO MY UNCLE CARL, WITH LOVE ...

I am doing what my heart tells me to do and I do it unstintingly.
—Carl Laemmle

Such was the heartfelt pledge of my uncle, Carl Laemmle in the granting of an estimated 300 affidavits of $10,000.00 each for persecuted Jewish refugees caught up in the reign of terror during the Nazi occupation of Germany in the 1930s. It was a time of torment and oppression.

Jewish property was plundered. Jewish assets could not be taken out of Germany.[10]

Carl Laemmle agonized over their plight and vowed to help as many as he could. It was a commitment from which he never wavered. Above and beyond Carl Laemmle's rise to fame and fortune, his merits as a caring, compassionate human being rate the highest. He never forgot his roots or his people. "It Can Be Done" became his running motto.

After Carl Laemmle sold Universal Studios he devoted the greater part of his time to the issuing of affidavits. It was a complicated, time consuming process. He was in a constant struggle with The State Department and their more ever exacting requirements. They had to have irrefutable proof that Carl Laemmle was capable of assuming so large an obligation.

Likewise, they required absolute assurance that aliens Carl Laemmle transported did not become public charges.

Carl Laemmle made every effort to comply with every demand. He gave sworn statements as to his assets, and pledged full responsibility for each affidavit recipient, plus his personal guarantee that not a single one of the beneficiaries would ever become public charge. All of these verbal battles with the State Department became draining and debilitating on my uncle Carl. It took a toll on his energy resources. The time eventually came when my uncle was no longer permitted to issue any more affidavits as he had already issued far too many. He then sought to find other sponsors. He wrote to his wealthy Jewish friends entreating them to pledge their own personal affidavits and give their utmost to the cause.

Carl Laemmle never let up his resolve and dedication in his humanitarian efforts for the remainder of his life. Carl Laemmle's legacy is a many faceted treasure trove of 20 years of "Carl Laemmle Presents"—reel upon reel of... "Mystery," "Adventure," "Horror," "Comedy," "Tragedy," "Romance," and "Fantasy." It is a "World of Imagination," a "World of Make-Believe."

But there is yet another facet to Carl Laemmle's legacy that relates to the stark reality of life and evil in this factual world we live in — and to a time in our not too distant past when a madman was formulating his diabolic plan — the extermination of the entire Jewish race.

By virtue of Carl Laemmle's innate humanity, magnanimity and life-saving affidavits, hundreds of imperiled German Jews and their families were given the chance to escape Nazi domination and seek refuge here in the United States.

Carl Laemmle was also a very loving, caring brother to my father and our family. I shall ever be grateful to him for the privilege of growing up on the Universal Studio lot and living all those magical years in that City of make-believe—an unforgettable time of my life.

Carl Laemmle's legacy lives on today in the lives of their children and their children's children. What greater legacy than the gift of life? I love you uncle Carl, Carla.

Looking back, Stanley Bergerman wrote the following:

I am deeply grateful that Carl Laemmle said 'yes" and became my father-in-law. I was privileged to have married his daughter, the delightful Rosabelle. Carl Laemmle's virtues were many. Here are a few. He was courageous, progressive and an adventurous leader and pioneer in the motion picture industry, founder and president of Universal. Uncle Carl, as most all of us called him, held out a helping hand not only to friends and family, but to strangers and newcomers seeking a break and a chance to enter pictures. His open door brought professional hope to discouraged people worn out by casting offices and unimagative producers and directors. He discovered many stars, directors and producers, including Irving Thalberg. Universal underwent vicissitudes in its long trek to becoming "a major," sometimes involving personal crisis. None were too big or too tough for this

Mission to Moscow (Warner Bros. 1943) is on the far right with her arm extended. She loved her work in "the musicals."

5'2"giant from Laupheim, Germany. I have watched Uncle Carl at the helm of Universal fixing grim problems with unfailing courage, precision and sharp judgment. Carl Laemmle guided good old "U" through the shoals to defy conspirators and predators.

Another star producer from Universal was Carl Laemmle, Jr., who brought to the screen such notable pictures as *All Quiet on the Western Front*, *Back Street*, *Dracula*, *Frankenstein* and *Strictly Dishonorable*. Bless Carl Laemmle—-I loved this man.

Over the course of the next six years the residents of 1749 North Mariposa Street were busy living, loving and learning. Carla appeared as a dancer in the following motion pictures: *The Chocolate Soldier* with Nelson Eddy and Risë Stevens (MGM, 1941), *Mission to Moscow* with Walter Huston and Anne Harding (Warner Bros., 1943), *Step Lively* with an all-star cast including Frank Sinatra, George Murphy (who later became Senator of California from 1964 through 1975), Adolphe Menjou, Walter Slezak, Eugene Pallette, comedians Carney and Brown,

Carla (left) with actor, George Murphy (and unknown showgirl) from the dance sequence, "Snakey Business" in RKO's *Step Lively* (1944).

Gloria DeHaven and Anne Jeffreys (RKO, 1944). Miss Jeffreys had also appeared with Carla in a Greek Theatre operetta, one of several performances in which Carla danced.

Dancing alongside Frank Sinatra in *Step Lively* was a joy for Carla and she remembers that he was a perfect gentleman. Had she forged any special bonds with Mr. Sinatra? Carla summed it all up this way:

Frank Sinatra and Anne Jeffreys to his right and Carla Laemmle during the filming of another dance number from *Step Lively* (RKO 1944).

> We were dancers, dancing in a motion picture. I was one in the dance troupe and always stayed with my troupe. We dancers stayed much to ourselves. As for myself, I did not associate with any Hollywood stars. That was taboo for many of us. We did our job and we went home. We, as dancers, formed bonds with our choreographers. The Greek Theatre days happened during this time and I had the pleasure of dancing on the same stage with Anne Jeffreys.

Carla said of working on films during the 1940s:

> Working in those motion pictures was one of the most marvelous times in my life. It wasn't easy, but we were surrounded by each other, a fine dance troupe of personalities. We had a common bond. And the choreographers were outstanding. George Balanchine, and Ernst Matray and his wife Maria are all unforgettable

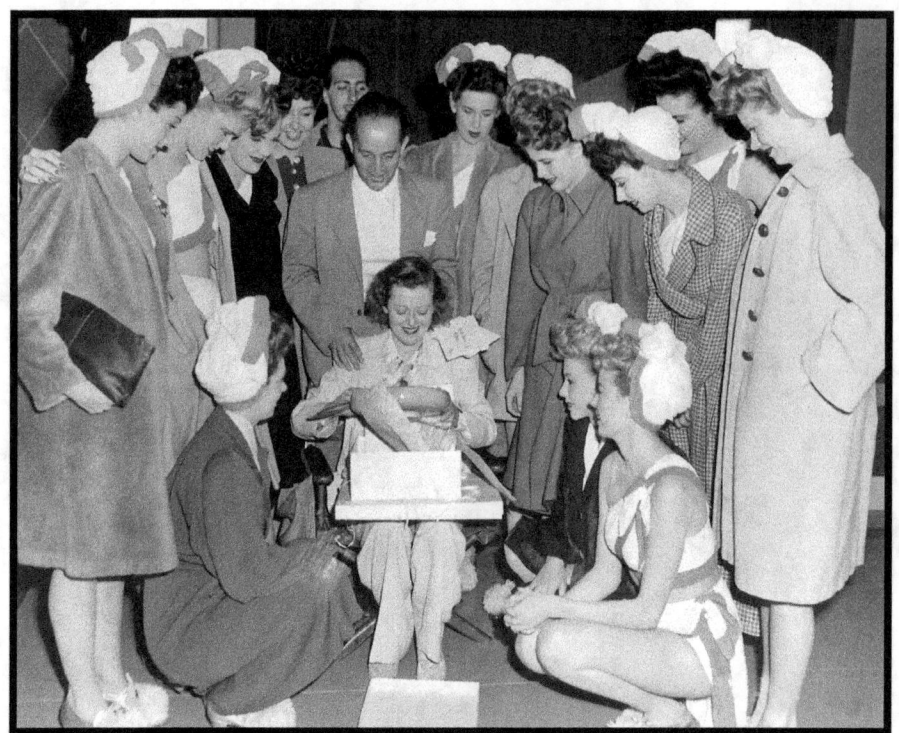

Choreographers, Ernest and his wife, Maria Matray as she opens a gift from the dancers who threw her a surprise birthday party after rapping on the set of *Step Lively* (RKO 1944). Carla stands second from right in checked robe.

to me. We had a surprise birthday party for Maria on the set of *Step Lively*.

Carla's mother Belle remained active in community events, including holding meetings with the Chinese Culture Society, of which Ray Cannon was also still an active member during the 1940s. On the professional side, Cannon's work in movies had decreased and in 1940 he was forced into bankruptcy. With WWII still raging, Ray applied for active duty, but in the fall of 1942 he was rejected by the Air Corps. His rejection letter was written by then 2nd Lieutenant, Ronald Reagan.

Junior Laemmle kept up Hollywood spirits by throwing lavish New Years Eve parties, many of which Carla attended. One party that she fondly remembers was New Years Eve 1940 when she was introduced to a young lady by the name of Evelyn Moriarty, who became a close friend of Laemmle, Jr.

Previously, Evelyn had been a model in New York before she worked as a showgirl for George White in his infamous stage production

George White's Scandals. Upon her arrival on the West Coast Evelyn was sent to see Earl Carroll. She had worked for two years at the nightclub bearing his name. Earl Carroll had nightclubs in both Hollywood and New York. The Carroll girls were astonishingly beautiful and personified the look of a modern young girl in the 1940s.[11] They were comparable to the Ziegfeld girls. Moriarty would be the stand-in for Marilyn Monroe in her last several films including *Let's Make Love* (1960), *The Misfits* (1961).

Evelyn Moriarty remained close friends with Junior Laemmle until his death. She and Carla Laemmle have remained friends since the day they first met. Carla said that of all the Hollywood luminaries she has known, her three lasting friendships were with Evelyn Moriarty; dancer and actress Barbara Perry, who had played a schoolgirl in *The Mystery of Edwin Drood*; and former child actress Edith Fellows, who had played Adele Rochester in 1934s *Jane Eyre* and later did a series of films starring as Polly Pepper.

Evelyn Moriarty and "Junior" Laemmle on a date in 1942.

Among the Rugged Peaks

Carla Laemmle (now under the professional name Carol Lenard) posing from left at bottom stairs in a dance number from *Night and Day* (Warner Bros., 1945).

The United States military dropped atomic bombs on the cities of Hiroshima and Nagasaki in the summer of 1945. The decision to drop the bombs was made by President Truman. Japan surrendered to the Soviet Union, Wednesday, August 15, 1945. WWII was officially over. Carla remembered when the war ended:

> It was quite a celebration. I was working at RKO in the movie version of *George White's Scandals* as a dancer with Jack Haley and Joan Davis. I worked again with the Matrays and we were all so happy to know that the war had finally come to an end. I remember, years later, reading in the newspaper that Ernst Matray had passed away. It is believed that he was the oldest surviving European choreographer until his death in Los Angeles at the age of 87. I was told that his wife is no longer living. [Maria Matray passed away in Munich, Germany October 1993.]

Carla's last major studio Hollywood film appearance was in Warner Bros.' *Night and Day* (1946), which starred Cary Grant as composer and lyricist Cole Porter. While the fighting was over over there, it was just beginning for workers trying to unionize the film studio workers. Hollywood's infamous Black Friday on October 5, 1945, delayed production on *Night and Day*. The month long set decorators strike took a dangerous turn when the strikers came up against armed police and studio goons at the front gate of Warner Bros. Over 40 people were injured. Carla said:

Snapshot of dancers from *Night and Day* (Warner Bros., 1945). Carla is standing at far right.

> Our dancing scenes with Alexis Smith were shot strictly at Warner Bros. I was no part of location shots that were added and Black Friday never personally affected me.

Ray Cannon directed *Samurai* in 1945—it would be his last Hollywood movie. He featured his friend, actor and martial artist David Chow (*Conquest of the Planet of the Apes* [1976] and *Bruce Lee: The True Story* [1976]) in his movie debut as a Japanese Secret Serviceman.[12] An overstressed Ray Cannon developed stomach ulcers and was advised by his doctors to "go fishing." Ray followed the advice, which literally changed his life. He began spending leisure time along the Pacific Coast of California. Mike Hager was one of Ray's first fishing buddies. Hager provided the vessel for the trips. Ray's knowledge and insight regarding the Baja, California peninsula became important to him.

In 1947 Ray visited San Felipe, which is located at the northern end of the Sea of Cortez. He was persuaded by another fishing buddy, character actor and opera singer, Eddie Abdo, (*Kismet* and *The Mummy's Curse*, both 1944) to let him in on the adventure. Ray once wrote:

> I have a special attachment for the North End of the Sea of Cortez, since it was there that I experienced a single, adventure-packed day that changed the whole course of my life. It was a day so filled with excitement and enchantment that it caused me to shed my lifetime career and become a vagabundo del mar—a vagabond of the sea—a way of life that sas given me many rewarding and fun crammed years. It was a rags to riches story in reverse. That day was my first on the bountiful and mysterious waters of the Sea of Cortez, and within a few hours I became involved in the most fantastic fishing I had ever experienced.

In 1948 Ray began to research fishing the pacific coast. Many fishing trips were undertaken, and finally Ray began writing about his experiences. While Ray was working on his first book, Carla was able to lend a hand because Ray needed someone to type his manuscript—he wrote everything by hand. Carla remembered:

> I knew nothing about typing but I knew I could learn to do it. I bought an old Remington from a neighbor and a friend gave me a little booklet entitled, *The Shortest Typing Course in the World*. It really proved to be that. I was typing in no time!

In addition to typing Ray's manuscript, Carla assisted in the scientific research, and more importantly, she drew over 160 fish identification illustrations for the book. When the book was finally completed, Ray took the manuscript and drawings to Lane Publishing Company. They seemed to be impressed—and they certainly were—the very next day Ray received a telegram announcing their decision to publish his book.

In the spring of 1949 Ray became critically ill from bleeding stomach ulcers. The prognosis was grim. There were no options but surgery. However, Ray had no health insurance and could not afford the operation. Carla recalled that though Ray's situation appeared desperate, he managed to maintain his Taoist calm as he awaited the solution to his problem, which came in a most miraculous way. She remembered:

Our dear and longtime friend and noted fashion designer, Cora Galenti, with the help of some very influential people, without delay, organized and staged a High Society Benefit Fashion Show Ball. It was a great success. Cora raised $5,000.00 for Ray's operation!

At the time, Carla was assisting Cora Galenti with a series of designer showings and meetings in Texas. At Cedars of Lebanon Hospital on Friday, March 4, 1949, Ray had a considerable portion of his stomach removed. It took several months of convalescence and TLC on both the part of Carla and her mother to get him back on his feet.

Carla's friend Cora Galenti (right), saved Ray's life in 1949 when she raised $5,000 for his ulcer operation. (From left) Carla's mother, Belle Laemmle, Carla, Ray, and Cora's son Anthony Palma, on leave during WWII.

Much of Ray's recuperation was due in part to the garden he kept in the backyard of the house on Mariposa. A letter from Ray in the summer of 1949 explains:

> My Sweet,
> The garden has never before expressed itself with so much luxuriance. As I walked there for a look of the day an amorous butterfly was waiting. T'was twilight and all the tiny people had long since sought their protective shelters. It settled on my hand and I noticed that no matter how I turned my hand it would move around, always facing me.
> As I surveyed the delightfulness of the growing, flowering, fruiting things, I wished my vision could be televised to you. I know how your heart would have been flooded with sheer joy. The sun-rouged cheeks of the

10-year anniversary gathering for the Chinese Culture Society. Ray Cannon is not present. (Second and third from right) Carla and mother Belle (1949).

peaches and ming-yellow blossoms flourishing among the guava vines match the brilliance of the evening star. The wholesome redness of the ripening tomatoes, jade-green fugwa hang and sway from their bamboo trapezes, now completely covered. All promise of goodness. Truly a garden of glory.

Quince must be canned in a day or so. Then the bushel or so of peaches. Had the first ripe one today. The second planting of beans is just beginning. I hope they last for you. I will soon plant lettuce, turnips and carrots. The broccoli is still flourishing; so is the squash, cucumbers, etc.,etc. The tomatoes are just ripening. All their vines took a second growth despite the early blight and have now reached the top wire. The cactus in your window box is beginning to send "out little sprouts." The sponge vines climbed all over the bamboo arbor and are now up to the porch roof.

> Day by day I gain strength and endurance. The only pain is in the emptiness and mysterious vacuum in my heart and arms for you.—Ray.

Death was no stranger to the Laemmle family during these times. Carrie E. Campbell, sister of the late Emogene Norton, aunt to Belle Laemmle, and Carla Laemmle's great-aunt, passed away at her home in Elizabeth, New Jersey, where she had lived for 22 years. Her death came on New Year's day 1948. She was a former Urbana, Illinois resident where she lived with her husband, James A. Campbell. Her daughter, Mrs. Grace Danielson, also survived her. Her body was transported to Urbana for burial at Mount Hope Cemetery. She was buried alongside her husband and parents at the age of 91.[13]

Soon after Aunt Carrie's death, Belle Laemmle suffered a small stroke that left her weakened. Her frequent trips to the library to study the family genealogy grew less and less. Next to Carla and Ray, this research was the one most important thing in her life. Unfortunately, after falling ill in 1948, she could never manage to continuously work on her genealogy. Although Belle continued to have small strokes throughout the remainder of her life, she remained socially active until 1957 in the DAR, Women's International Peace Crusade, National Society Daughters of the Union, Daughters of the American Colonists and United Defenders of the Four Freedoms.

The 1950s began with adjustments for both Carla Laemmle and Ray Cannon. Fortunately, Ray had recovered from his life threatening illness and continued his beloved gardening. He was also learning more about the Baja California coast while he and Carla continued to work on their book. In 1953, after nearly five years of work, *How to Fish the Pacific Coast* was published. It became known as "the fisherman's bible."[14]

Belle Laemmle was in her 79th year. Mrs. Laemmle's health was not the best for the last 12 years of her life. Carla recalls:

> My mother wasn't able to go out on her own as much as she had. I would take her to her DAR meetings now and then. She enjoyed reading and watching television.

The summer of 1950 saw the United States involved in war once again. The success of the Chinese Revolution was followed by

Carla (second from left) in publicity shot for the new Paris Inn on Broadway Avenue in Los Angeles (1951).

the outbreak of the Korean War.[15] Once again war would affect the economy. In Hollywood steady work was difficult to find for Carla Laemmle. Dancing was her chosen profession and major source of income. She now needed to find another outlet for her dancing other than motion pictures. She auditioned for dance agent Lottie Horner, who booked small groups of dancers into nightclubs. Horner signed her taking Carla's career in a different direction.

As fate would have it, Lottie had a booking already lined up for a group of six dancers at the newly relocated Paris Inn near Chinatown on North Broadway Avenue.[16] Although Carla was past the age of 40, she looked like a girl half her age. Ultimately, Carla became one of the six Parisianettes, who danced in colorful, elaborate costumes from the Naughty Nineties to the Roaring Twenties.

In addition to performing with the Parisianettes chorus line, Carla had her own specialty numbers ranging from comedy dance routines to interpretive dances such as the Viennese Waltz. She was the only professionally trained dancer in the group and served as a choreographer whenever she was needed. Carla remembered:

Working at the Paris Inn was certainly a different life from Hollywood. It was exciting, non-stop! I loved working there. It was a creative and fun time of my life. The people there were so friendly and we got to know all the regulars. It was part of our job, as the Parisianettes to socialize with the patrons when invited. I never drank, and I had an understanding with the bartender never to serve me any hard liquor. Paris Inn was also a very fine restaurant. We had a still photographer around at all times. If a customer chose they would be photographed with the entertainment or with each other. Their photographs came immediately in a decorative sleeve. That would be a souvenir from their experience at the Paris Inn. Another innovation was their singing waiters, who sang classic Opera arias between shows. You can see by the photographs that it was quite a showplace.

It was during the run of the Paris Inn engagement that Donald Davis came into my life, an event culminating in the unthinkable, my betrayal of Ray and subsequent fall from grace. I had tried to block it all from my memory and somewhat succeeded. I never expected to reveal any of it. How was I to tell it now? I feel that my readers would be shocked and would hate me. My first thought was to delete the entire sequence of events from this biography. That would leave me pure and untarnished. But it would also be evading the truth and tantamount to lying. I could not do that. I shall therefore tell the story as it played out, however harshly my readers wish to judge me. It all began one evening when a handsome young serviceman named Donald Davis made his appearance at the Paris Inn. He had come up from his base in San Diego where he was awaiting orders for deployment to the War with Korea. Donald had a very charming, outgoing personality and joined in the merriment at the Paris Inn by playing his guitar and singing to the audience who loved it. It was pretty obvious that Donald was attracted to me right from the first evening. He was so handsome and charming, I was flattered by the attention.

Merriment at the Paris Inn. Carla is "Parisianette," second from left (1951).

As Donald became a more frequent patron of the Paris Inn, it was apparent that our relationship had turned a notch more romantic. He began writing to me. His letters to me were so romantic. I loved the attention. But not for a moment was I taking it seriously. After all, Donald was 20 years younger than I! Besides, Ray Cannon was the love of my life and while Ray then had to be away a lot gathering material for his book, *How to Fish the Pacific Coast*, Ray and I had a very special and meaningful 18-year bond together! At this time, Ray knew nothing about my little dalliance with Donald. I saw no reason to tell him as nothing would ever come of it. How wrong I was! I couldn't have misjudged it more!

In the meantime, the other Parisianettes in the group were going gaga over Donald's intense romance for me. They ganged up on me. They wouldn't let me alone and kept messing with my emotions. I began to wonder if I really might be having deeper feelings for Donald than I realized. What was going on with me? Somewhere during this time I may have mentioned something about Donald to Ray.

Carla with Donald Davis (1952).

One night Donald brought his mother, who lived in San Francisco, to the Paris Inn to meet me. I liked her a lot. We had such nice conversation. If only she had been honest with me about Donald, this would be a very different story.

Donald's remaining time at his base in San Diego was nearing its end and he would be leaving for Korea. He kept pleading his love for me, that he was an American patriot soon to be going to war and possibly never to return. He passionately pressured me into marriage.

I had no thoughts as to the rational of it. I was swept away by the romance and drama of it. 'Yes, Yes!' I would marry Donald! My feelings for Ray were no longer in the equation.

I was in such a fragile state of mind at an irresponsible time of my life, 54 years ago. My engagement as a Parisianette had come to a close. The die was cast! One night, after Ray had left on another one of his fishing trips, I did the unforgivable. I walked out on my frail and loving mother and left with Donald for Las Vegas! I have no memory of what I told my mother as to where we were going or planning to do. Whatever was too painful, I simply blocked out. I had previously arranged with my good friend, Cora Galenti, to set up a little apartment in the valley for Donald and I to stay briefly after our marriage. Donald was sent to Korea just after the second week. The whole time period after our return from Las Vegas is hazy to me. I do not remember when I called home and talked to my mother or to Ray.

I was happy when I was home again and hoped that things could somehow get back to normal. I knew I had hurt Ray beyond all forgiveness, not to mention what I did to my dear mother. I also knew that Ray still needed me for the completion of *How To Fish the Pacific Coast* book.

Psychologically, at the time, I was living in a kind of romanticized dream world of my own making. It wasn't to be for long, however. I was puzzled as to why I had not received any notification from the War Department in regard to the allotment that I was due to receive as a newly married wife of a serviceman on active duty. I wrote to the War Department but never got an answer.

It was then that I wrote to Donald's mother to tell her about our recent marriage in Las Vegas and got the shock of my life! She phoned to tell me that Donald was already a married man and had three children! I was stunned! She said that she had promised Donald not to tell me that he was married. She was so very sorry. She asked me to forgive her.

If that wasn't enough, Donald had gone AWOL from the service. Two service officers came looking for him one night, but he wasn't with me. He had taken my car and was gone! About a week later, I got a call from the police department. They had found my car in Las Vegas but not Donald. Ray went to Las Vegas, soon after to pick up my car. Ray was absolutely wonderful about it all. I believe that Ray knew from the beginning that my marriage to Donald was doomed and that I would come to my senses one day. I was free at last from the hypnotic trance I felt that I had been under.

I got an annulment and never saw Donald again. I tossed out all of his letters to me as well as the marriage certificate and annulment. I didn't want any evidence or record of the worst mistake of my life. I don't know if Donald is still alive, in prison, or dead! I had kept in touch with Donald's mother for a while. She told me about the pain and sorrow Donald brought into her life and that she couldn't take it any more and had legally disowned him. Finally, it was Ray's unconditional love, understanding and acceptance that truly brought me a healing sense of inner peace and redemption.

In 1953 the rented house at 1749 Mariposa was being sold and the Laemmle family was asked to move. Ray's and Carla's friend Mike Hager happened to see a house on Serrano Avenue that was for rent in the Old Hollywood area. The owner was a banker who lived in Long Beach. He and his son had the house built in the late 1920s. The property actually housed three structures, the home, a smaller guesthouse and a garage. For Ray, Mrs. Laemmle and Carla, this would be their last move.

In the summer of 1953 the Korean War ended and on June 11 Carla's Uncle Siegfried Laemmle passed away at the age of 90. He was the eldest surviving Laemmle brother. His brother Louis, the last surviving of the Carl Laemmle brothers, passed away February 12, 1956 at age 86.

This photo created such a stir in 1928 that Uncle Carl had all photos and negatives destroyed but this one that was saved by Carla.

Carla Laemmle, for personal posterity had nude photos taken of herself, which she paid to have taken. It was during this time she took accepted a job in which she modeled women's undergarments as Carol Lenard; this semi-nude was photographed in the 1950s.

This year would also be Ray Cannon's year for a rebirth. Ray's book, *How to Fish the Pacific Coast* was finally published, which coincided with the premiere publication of *Western Outdoor News*—"The only state-wide sportsmen's newspaper published in California." The fledgling resort owners of Baja California were desperately in need of publicity and the premieres of the book and magazines could not have occurred at a more opportune time. This was definitely a second calling for Ray Cannon. Carla remembers:

> Ray and I worked diligently, day and night on his first book. I began drawing the fish illustrations and Ray thought that was an absolutely wonderful addition. It was Ray's belief that when they saw my illustrations that's what really sold them on the idea. They accepted it and published the book. Ray received an $8,000 royalty check. In those days it was like eight million!

A featured article by Ray Cannon ran in the first issue of *Western Outdoor News*. Its owner, Burt Twilegar had worked as the outdoors editor for the *Los Angeles Examiner*. He and his (then) business partner, Earl H. "Tex" Hardage, launched the first issue that December 4, 1953. Ray was asked by Mr. Twilegar to write full time for his publication. Ray accepted his offer. Since Ray's weekly column would mainly be devoted to Pacific coast fishing, it would serve as a perfect showcase for his newly published book. Thus began for Ray and *Western Outdoor News* a productive and rewarding 25-year association. Carla remembered:

> By 1954, I was no longer working in stage and movies. I was now typing all of Ray's weekly columns as well as his growing correspondence. I called myself "Ray's secretary." I found the work very pleasurable for a total of 24 years. Ray would later expand his area of fishing to south of the border and explore the entire Baja California coast; the rich and primitive region of the Sea of Cortez.[17]

Belle Laemmle was soon to be 90 years of age—Carla threw her mother a 90th birthday party on February 23, 1961. It was a happy gathering of close friends although Belle wished that her cousin, Grace Campbell Danielson, could have attended. Grace, one of the last surviving members of Belle's family, was 70 years of age and living in New Jersey with her husband. Belle received many birthday cards including one from Grace and another memorable card from the members of the Chinese Culture Society. In addition Belle received a handwritten note from her niece and nephew, Rosabelle and Junior Laemmle as follows:

Rosabelle Laemmle Bergerman (1901-1965).

Dear Aunt Belle,
I'm sorry we missed your birthday celebration—a very wonderful occasion. Our heartiest congratulations even though a little belated. So difficult to know what you'd like, but Jr. and I would like you to have a little remembrance from us. I am sure Carla will be better able

> to choose something that's right, so we are enclosing a little remembrance for you. Fondly, Rosabelle & Carl, Jr. [who signed "Merry Birthday, Love, Junior"]

Belle Laemmle's life came to an end in Los Angeles, California on Tuesday, March 11, 1962. Her life revolved around her husband and family and she had been a proud wife and mother. Mrs. Laemmle had experienced many changes in her 91 years, including 18 presidencies. Her mother, Emma Norton lived through 22 presidencies. Belle's death came 400 years from the day that her first female descendant, Bridget Allgar was born, in Shalford, Essex, England. Bridget Allgar was the mother of Mary White. Mary White was the wife of Joseph Loomis (one of the first English colonial settlers and descendant of Belle Norton), thus perpetuating the Loomis family tree. Mrs. Joseph Laemmle, was a proud American who shared her heritage with others. In 1954, the Peyton Randolph Chapter of the *Daughters of the American Revolution* "affectionately" dedicated their Year Book to Carrie Belle Norton Laemmle, their proud 50-year member. Her gentle spirit continued to inspire others.

Carla remembered the months before that lead up to her mother's death:

> It was after Christmas 1961 when I first put my mother in a nursing home. I visited her everyday, but after a few weeks she was mentally getting out of control. Her doctor made arrangements to send her to Los Angeles County Hospital [now called Los Angeles County USC Medical Center]. They gave her absolutely wonderful care. I drove down to see her almost everyday. I felt bad that I couldn't take care of her at home but it was more than I could handle. She was at the hospital for three months before she passed away there. She was a dear, kind and wonderful mother, and everybody who knew her loved her as the very gentle lady that she was.

The assassination of President John F. Kennedy in Dallas, Texas in 1963 had the nation stunned. Lyndon Baines Johnson immediately became the 36th President of the United States. Hubert H. Humphrey then became the Vice-president. Carla, like most Americans, remembers where she was that Friday, November 22, 1963:

> What a shock! I was right here at home. I heard about it on the television. Ray was in Baja California at the time. I had previously planned a dinner. I invited my cousin, Carol Bergerman [she was Carl Laemmle's only granddaughter then a woman of 33] and her boyfriend, Chuck. Carol called to ask me if I was going to go ahead with the dinner. I said yes. We sat around the television in disbelief before we finally had dinner that evening. I remember that the following Thursday was Thanksgiving. We celebrated that Thanksgiving at home. Ray had returned from his trip and I had invited several "loners" over for dinner. Among them was our good friend, Bill Burke.

Carla's relationship with Bill Burke became another unforgettable chapter in her life. She remembered:

> I first met Bill back in 1958 while attending an Esoteric class, "Thinking and Destiny," which was based on the book by Harold W. Percival. Our mutual passion for the great mystical teachings of the East formed the basis for our friendship. I looked forward to introducing Bill to Ray, as I believed they were in true accord on many levels.

Bill Burke was a highly qualified electronic engineer who was working for Lockheed during this time. When his employment ended in 1961, Ray Cannon asked Burke if he would like to try his hand at drawing some maps for *The Sea of Cortez,* the book that Cannon was writing. Bill undertook the assignment with the utmost enthusiasm and put every bit of his know how into this project.[18]

During the long months of meticulous work, Burke spent many hours with Ray Cannon at the house, and consequently also with Carla, who developed a close relationship with Burke. In fact, it was much more than just a friendship—they had fallen in love. Ray Cannon's attitude

Carla with William "Bill" Burke (1962).

toward Carla and Bill's growing attachment to one another was true Taoist acceptance. Carla explained her feelings at the time:

> It wasn't that my deep feelings for Ray had grown less. It was simply that the romantic aspect of our 26-year relationship had changed over the course of time. One of the delightful qualities I loved about Bill was that he was a true romantic at heart. One night we were having dinner at one of our favorite restaurants. We ordered marguerites as usual and made a toast. What an unforgettable and romantic moment it was for me to find a diamond engagement ring in the bottom of my cocktail glass! Not long after that eventful evening one of our good friends threw an engagement party for us.

At that time, Carla had no real knowledge of the dark side of Bill Burke's nature. Sadly, she was about to learn that Bill suffered from bipolar disorder, and that he had attempted suicide more than once. Nonetheless, Carla was in love and accepted his difficulties. But it was Bill who was not accepting of himself. His temper and rages ruined their relationship. Carla remembered:

On one occasion, Bill and I had gone on a trip to Yosemite National Park. We were enjoying the adventure, laughing and having a happy time when Bill suddenly asked me if I brought along a certain sexy nightgown. I told him that since the weather was so cold that I hadn't. He went into a complete temper tantrum. Of course, the evening was ruined. It was a disaster. I slept in the car that night. However, the next morning I tried to pass it off. The rest of our stay was strained and joyless. Then there was that ill-fated evening I was visiting Bill at his apartment, a mile or so from the house. We were conversing amicably when out of the blue an argument ensued over Bill's false accusations that Ray was influencing me against him. It was getting ugly and I didn't want to deal with it. I just up and left and walked home. I found Ray seated in his chair watching television, as usual. I began to explain what had happened. Suddenly, I heard someone at the door. It was Bill, I assumed, coming to apologize. It was Bill, yes, but no! He was in an absolute rage and dashed over to where Ray was sitting and began hitting him over the head! I remember, to this day leaping over in front of Ray to shield him from Bill. It was a bad, sad and sorry scene. By this time, Bill knew that nothing was going to work between us. I had come to that realization much earlier. Nevertheless, I loved Bill. It was hard to give up on it. I had once even considered the totally illogical arrangement that the three of us, Bill, Ray and I could amicably live together under one roof! How could I have ever seriously considered such a solution possible?

Bill had many wonderful qualities but his illness hit him hard and I just could not deal with it. I could accept the reality of having no other love by my side. What mattered most of all was having Ray in my life. For Bill, I am sure, he felt that dark world closing in on him. No job, no available work, no money and the tension over our relationship and our break-up. I was deeply concerned and unhappy over the situation.

November 22, 1968 – Bill Burke, Carla and Ray Cannon (who approved of Carla's relationship with Bill.) Standing among Ray's many fishing trophies that were on display at a Los Angeles hotel.

In the spring of 1970, Bill Burke informed Carla that he was going to San Diego for a job interview. She felt somewhat uneasy and didn't quite believe him. Bill left his car in Carla's driveway and she expected him back the following Saturday for dinner at the house. Saturday came, but Bill did not. Carla knew something was wrong.

After waiting 24 hours and hearing no word from Burke, Carla went to his apartment. Since she had no key she had to find the landlady's apartment and ask for help. The landlady was not eager to let Carla into the apartment, but she finally relented. Carla's worst fear was realized— Bill was lying fully dressed on his bed and was past anyone's help. The police were called and found he had overdosed on drugs. Burke had left no written note behind. William Joseph Burke's death certificate reads that he died Saturday, April 11, 1970.

Friday April 17, 1970, Ray Cannon wrote the following tribute to Bill Burke. It was later published in *Western Outdoor News*

LESSON IN COURAGE

For the past 12 years, I have repeatedly mentioned in this column Aero-Designer-Engineer, Bill Burke, a very close friend of Carla and myself, as having been on many happy fishing trips with us, somewhere along the California coast or in the Cortez. Or reported about mapping or other work he did for me in *The Sea of Cortez*. Bill's M.D. was a well-kept secret, but about a month ago, he told our close amigo that he had a transmigration appointment with his Karma in three weeks. Last Saturday, he quietly went to sleep and moved on.

During those three twilight weeks, Bill gave us no sign of his date with Destiny. He spent every evening with us with no letdown in his usual wit and humor, and eagerness to help do a share of the chores. I have never seen such a day after day courage. The lesson I learned from it may prove my greatest gain from observing human behavior. After much profound thought, I hope to sit down and write a philosophical projection of that courage. Bill's many fishing friends will long remember another side of Bill's life, his youthful enthusiasm [he was 45] and praise of the art and sport of fishing. Bill's "Radiant Shores" must provide the best fishing in the Firmament.

Carla wrote the following in a letter to one of Bill's four sisters:

Your letters are much appreciated and so very comforting... I mentioned that Bill had taped several sessions that he had with a psychiatrist (the tapes were left in the trunk of his car). It was only this morning that I felt able to play one or two of them. It was, of course, a painful thing to listen to. The main thread running through conversations was the recurring urge that periodically would sweep over Bill—to commit suicide. An urge which he fought against for 18 years, according to the tapes...He felt I no

Ray and Carla (February 1970).

longer loved him and wanted to be free to find someone else...He said that he hated himself and wanted to destroy his only enemy—himself. As I listened to his words, I couldn't help feeling that I failed to communicate with him when he needed it most...I know there is nothing that can be changed now and it is senseless torturing myself. I must learn to accept change, in all its many forms. This

world is not permanent, nor anyone in it. We must all learn to let go. This is a difficult lesson, as we all get so "caught up" with life. Detachment is the secret, but to practice it is another thing.
My love and gratitude, Carla.

Regarding Bill Burke's death, Carla concluded:

For a very long time I felt responsible for Bill's suicide. It was psychologically devastating to me. I loved him. I've thought a lot about Bill's death. No one knows for sure why someone takes his or her own life. But I've come to accept the circumstances.

The Laemmle family would mourn another loss, the death of Carl Laemmle's daughter, Carla's cousin, Rosabelle Laemmle Bergerman. Carla said:

I thought a great deal of Rosabelle. She was very warm-hearted. We had a nice rapport. She was very loving to me and I loved her dearly. She was also very fluent in the German language. One almost would have to be. She accompanied her father, my uncle, on several trips to Europe. She also looked after and stood by him and was a fine and fun hostess at many of the Hollywood parties. She planned many of those parties that Carl Laemmle had back in those days.

In 1929, when Rosabelle married Stanley Bergerman, Carla played part in the wedding party. Carla remembered:

That was a proud day for my Uncle Carl to see his daughter marry. In the years since their marriage, I watched Rosabelle's children, Carol and Stanley Jr. grow up. They lived in Beverly Hills and I didn't get to see much of her then. Holiday parties were when we got to see each other most. One of the things that I remember most about Rosabelle is that she had the sexiest woman's voice I had

Ray and Carla fishing on the Sea of Cortez (1970).

ever heard. I miss her dearly. Her husband, Stanley and I became closer after Rosabelle's death. Stanley remarried. His new wife Fay, was just as charming. Fay and Stanley would ask me to go to the Dorothy Chandler Pavilion for concerts. He loved music. He always had season tickets. Carol, Rosabelle's daughter loved music too. I also went with Carol to the Dorothy Chandler a few times.

In the years that followed the publication of *The Sea of Cortez*, Ray continued writing and Carla continued to type Ray's weekly columns for *Western Outdoors News*. Ray made frequent trips to Baja California and organized small Sea of Cortez voyages. Carla accompanied Ray on three occasions. They also visited the beautiful cities of Baja's Mulege, Rancho Buena Vista and La Paz. They also visited the Mexican city of Xochimilco and traveled to the very tip of Baja. Carla remembered:

> It was all so adventurous and exciting. Soon after, Ray starred in a television special entitled, *Cannon of*

the Cortez for Wolper Productions. He had in mind to write a sequel to *The Sea of Cortez*. It was to be about the intriguing Vagabundos del Mar, the strange and fascinating sea-roving Nomads of the Cortez.

Ray and Carla spent the years happily together, writing and traveling. Carla specifically remembers the months prior to the summer of 1977:

> It was in the fall of 1976, when we outright bought the house here on Serrano. Soon thereafter, I had a premonition that all was not well with Ray. I couldn't quite put my finger on it but it cast a dark shadow over me. When Ray returned from the World Festival of Fishing in Rancho Buena Vista [his home away from home] in November of 1976, what was to be his final trip to the Cortez, he appeared exhausted. His color had an unhealthy grayish hue. I couldn't shake the ominous feeling I had that Ray was gravely ill. When I asked him how he was he only said he'd had some headaches due to a severe sunstroke while in Baja. Ray eventually got back in the groove of writing his weekly column and even making plans for another small boat voyage to the Midriff Islands of the Cortez, come June.
>
> While I tried to be supportive of his plans, the premonition that Ray would not be with me much longer cast a heavy pall over me. It was a constant ache in my heart. Sadly, my fears were borne out. Ray never made that last small boat voyage to the Midriff Islands. He passed away, Tuesday, June 7, 1977 of brain cancer. He was 84.

The Los Angeles funeral services for Raymond Cannon were held Saturday, June 11, 1977 at the Utter McKinley Wilshire Chapel at two o'clock p.m. Rev. Manly Palmer Hall officiated. Among those who paid their respects were Helen and Jimmy Dietrich, Burt Twilegar, Carol Bergerman and Ruthe Kanakoff. Printed on Ray's memorial card was the following "Fisherman's Prayer":

God grant that I may live to fish
Until my dying day.
And when it comes to my last cast,
I then most humbly pray,
 When in the Lord's safe landing net
I'm peacefully asleep.
That in His Mercy I be judged
As big enough to keep,

Western Outdoor News ran a cover photo of Ray Cannon in their June 17, 1977 issue. Editor and owner, Burt Twilegar wrote a tribute to Ray.[19] The following was excerpted from that tribute:

> He's made hundreds of trips to Baja. He's led the fun loving Vagabundos del Mar on numerous boat cruises around the Peninsula. He's fished for and caught almost everything that swims in the Sea of Cortez. He's been shipwrecked and lived off the land.

Ray's death was also given notice in *Variety Weekly*, June 22. In the June 24th issue of *Western Outdoor News* (page 6), Carla Laemmle wrote the following tribute to Ray in the last column that bore his name. It was entitled "He Enjoyed Life to the Fullest:"

> TO THE MANY FRIENDS who knew Ray, there is little doubt in my mind that most all of them would agree that he qualified to fit the term, "unforgettable character." He was truly an "original," a one of a kind. To me, who was fortunate enough to have been with Ray over half my lifetime, he was all that and much, much, more. I knew a side of his nature and philosophy of life that others were not aware of.
> Of course he enjoyed thoroughly his image of being the salty "old man of the Sea of Cortez" having a crowd of his readers and admirers around him listening enthralled to his captivating story telling, and belly laughing at his sprightly humor. Ray was a born actor and knew well how to dramatize a story. He was, of course, a superb

Another dream realized for Carla, the sequel to *The Sea of Cortez*, published in 1998.

writer, especially so in his lyrical phrasing and coloring which flowed so exquisitely and easily from his mind and pen.

DURING HIS EARLY days in motion pictures while doing some research work on *Broken Blossoms* for D.W. Griffith, Ray became interested in the study of Buddhism and other Oriental philosophies. He was particularly attracted to the mystical teachings of the ancient Chinese

Sage, Lao-tse, a philosophy called Taoism. It influenced him greatly. Later on Ray went to China and spent six months in a Buddhist Monastery, studying. It changed his whole approach to life

Taoism has been termed "The Quiet Way." It is a philosophy of "effortlessness," harmony and happiness; observing and following Nature's things, and the forever-moving-motion everywhere present in all things, and the quiet acceptance of that motion as change in our own life, ever seeking out the good and the beautiful, and adhering to the First Law: "Harm no one, especially yourself."

Ray truly believed by this quiet, gentle and happy philosophy. He enjoyed life to the fullest, and was always aware of it at the time. Through him, my own life has been greatly enriched. He taught me how to store the beauty of a sunset, a flower or work of art within my "memory bank" so it would never be lost. He made me mindful of the myriads of small lives around us, unseen, in Nature's Kingdom, each fulfilling its own simple and rightful destiny in the Allness of Tao.

RAY TAUGHT ME what it means to always keep the "child heart" and never lose that sense of "wonder" in the commonplace as well as in the mysteries of life. An ancient Chinese Proverb Ray sought to live by was "Make the many happy, expecting no reward.

I am grateful to have played a part and shared in the success of Ray's two beautiful books and to have contributed to his well being and happiness during our 42 years together. And I say from my heart, in all of the comings and goings and living and doing, Ray was the most fun to be with.

I believe I will feel the warmth of Ray's presence whenever I see a beautiful sunset, a hillside vista, or a landscape off some "way-out" island in his beloved Sea of Cortez. And because I have stored within me so much of the beauty that was Ray, he will never be lost to me.

I love you Ray dear, Carla.

Act Three:
MOVING FORWARD IN LIFE

Adapting to life without Ray was the hardest thing that Carla ever had to do. Ray was Carla's greatest inspiration throughout their 42-year relationship.

> Ray's death was a totally devastating, life-changing, life-shattering event for me. My own life had been such an integral part of his. I felt that my whole world had collapsed. But I had to be strong and hold myself together. There were further arrangements to be made with Baja California officials in La Paz for special services there, and most important, for the final ceremonial casting of Ray's ashes into the Sea of Cortez. Friday, June 24, 1977 was so terribly emotional, dramatic and surreal...the final plane ride to La Paz, the Mexican Wake ceremony in La Paz, the poignant boat ride to Isla Cerralvo and lastly, my casting of Ray's ashes off Cerralvo Island on the waters of his beloved Sea of Cortez. All are indelibly engraved in my heart.

"Sênôr Cannon" was considered the "Father of Baja." In July, following Ray's funeral, his portrait along with various mementos were placed in the National Archives of Mexico, at La Paz. Hubbs-Sea World Research Institute in San Diego, California honored Ray's memory with a fund for scientific research on the area he knew and loved so well.

Carla's own health was poor upon her return from Mexico.

> When it was over and I arrived back home I felt physically and emotionally drained and strangely weak. I assumed it was a reaction to the recent events I'd been through. It was in the month of August when I did not realize that I had a bleeding ulcer.
> In the days that followed I was not getting any stronger, but weaker. At some point I realized that I needed help. I called my neighbor, Ruthe to come over. She found

me unconscious on the bathroom floor. She gave me mouth-to-mouth resuscitation and called emergency. The paramedics came and rushed me to Hollywood Hospital [now Queen of Angels] since it was the closest. On the way there I suffered a massive hemorrhage. I only had a pint of blood left when we got to the hospital! I came close to joining Ray that day.

It was a lethal combination of stress and a powerful steroid drug I was taking and my negligence in not following my doctor's orders to *"always take food along with it."* That caused the lining of my stomach to become so thin it finally tore open. I had seven blood transfusions and remained in intensive care for three days. I later had to undergo surgery. It was all a very close call for me. I realized that I would have to get hold of my emotions or it would destroy me. Just to go back a few years, my neighbor Ruthe came to live in the little rental house in the rear of the property in the early 1970s. I might not be here today were it not for Ruthe Kanakoff. The fact is, Ruthe saved my life! I feel that my Karma and Ruthe's are definitely intertwined.

In 1999, after a series of illnesses, Ruthe moved closer to her daughter in Idaho—she had lived in Los Angeles since she was 14. Ruthe passed away Monday, July 7, 2003. She was 81. Carla wrote the following as a tribute to her friend:

What can I say about my dear friend Ruthe? She was an original in so many ways. She was highly gifted as a designer of unique jewelry and all manner of quaint irresistible collectibles. She was quietly spiritual and was a natural born psychic. She always had a lighted candle in her living room that radiated and projected an aura of protection. Plants and flowers too were likewise a vital part of her world. But Ruthe's love and compassion for all members of the animal kingdom were boundless. She, along with her numerous "what you see is what you get" feline tenants, and an occasional under-house guest raccoon were welcome at Ruthes.

My earliest memories of Ruthe centers around her passionate love of Nature, both the seen and the unseen Beauty around us. The spiders weaving their webs and the myriads of other small life engaged in their own little destinies.

There was "Big Daddy", a longhaired, black Persian cat that Ruthe adored for many years. Then at some point in time, "Tidbit", an aristocratic Russian Blue cat came into Ruthe's life one day. Tidbit was a savvy cat and immediately recognized a soft touch when she felt one. As time went by, the day arrived when Big Daddy made the final transition into the next dimension and Tidbit had unequivocally become my cat. Fast forward to the year 1985. An opportunity presented itself too irresistible to pass up and I took full advantage of it. I brazenly invited myself along with Ruthe and two other members of her family to attend the wedding of Ruthe's son to a lovely Japanese girl. They were to be married in Kyoto, Japan. I did, of course, pay all my share of the expenses, or whatever the cost.

Ruthe most graciously agreed. After all, what could she do? I was her landlady! The wedding was serene and beautiful. It took place at a Temple in Kyoto in the traditional Japanese manner. It was an exquisite ceremony and it was thrilling to me to be able to share in it. The following day we visited a number of incredibly beautiful Japanese gardens. We also visited the great parks, Temples, lakes and lagoons with many colorful fish. Ruthe and I found Tokyo to be a fascinating City. The Japanese have an exquisitely inborn sense of beauty. They make use of every space. They also plant exotic trees in the middle of their downtown streets! The accent on beauty is everywhere. Wherever a flower or fern could grow you will find one. Of course, everyone knows how creatively and tastefully they serve their food!

Enchanting is the word for Japan and its culture. After our time in Tokyo, I had previously made arrangements for Ruthe and me to go to the fabulous City of Hong Kong. I had a cousin who worked in a bank there and he was making all the arrangements for us. Hong Kong is like New Years Eve everyday! It is an exotic Bazaar of everything under the sun and all other planets combined! Ruthe and I both agreed, there is no place else like Hong Kong. Truly, Hong Kong is an addiction!

My cousin, Mark entertained us like Royalty. He arranged for us to have a most grandiose dinner in one of the private dining rooms of Hong Kong's upscale luxury hotels. And what a banquet it was! We were served and waited on by several traditionally dressed male and female servants who stood by at a respectable distance the entire time. They awaited our every beckoned call. They made us feel so important we almost began to believe it. What an unforgettable trip for us both!

But wait! It isn't over yet! In November of that same year, Ruthe and I joined a small tour group. Along with Ruthe's sister, we went on a fantastic combination trip to China and Egypt. It included a cruise on the Nile! All of it was absolute wonderment!

In China, we climbed The Great Wall, visited Imperial Palaces and ancient tombs of the former Kings, traveled down a great Boulevard bordered on either side with huge carved stone animals of every kind. We witnessed hundreds of young and old of both sexes as they gathered daily in parks and open Squares to practice their graceful and ancient art of Ti Chi exercises. It was such a delightful and amazing sight. Last but not least we enjoyed the divine Chinese concoctions, a treat for even the most blasé palate. Ruthe and I agreed that China was a total delight on every level.

Our Egypt and the Nile excursion was pure enchantment for both of us. It was like going back in time. We sailed up the Nile, just as it was thousands of years ago. Being in the very presence of the Pyramids built by the ancient Egyptians as a royal tomb and touching the remnants of the once great Palaces of "Rameses the Great" was thrilling. The Past was not dead here. The Glory of Egypt was all around us.

> We found Cairo an intriguing and fascinating City. With the winding, narrow streets and enticing seductive shops, on one hand, and a bustling modern Metropolis on the other; I couldn't resist buying an elegant Galabaya, the traditional Egyptian dress, and a couple of blouses. The Piece de Résistance of my shopping was a black and gold embroidered chiffon Galabaya and wrap that I still wear to this day to oohs and aahs! What a memorable year it was with a lifetime of cherished memories for both of us!
>
> It is my belief, as well as it was Ruthe's that death is but a transition, a release of the spirit from a worn-out physical body. Ruthe and I have a bond. We shall surely meet again.

In the summer of 1978, after recuperating from the ulcer surgery, Carla learned of a devastating family tragedy. Laura Lee Bergerman, the 18-year-old daughter of her second cousin Stanley Bergerman, Jr., was killed in an automobile accident. Carla remembered:

> Apparently, she had just graduated from high school and went with some friends to Tijuana, Mexico. She was a passenger in a van riding without a seatbelt. The van crashed and Laura Lee was thrown from the vehicle. She died instantly. This was devastating for everyone. She was such a young and beautiful child. Laura Lee's death was a terrible tragedy. It was all so sad.
>
> The tragedy was more than my cousin, Carol Bergerman, Laura Lee's Aunt, could take. She suffered an emotional breakdown over her niece's death. Much of her time was spent with Laura Lee. Carol had no children. In fact, at one point in time, Carol was Laura Lee's legal and temporary guardian. I 'm sure Carol never got over it.

As the years passed, Carla naturally began losing more and more friends and family. In the fall of 1979, she received a phone call from her friend Evelyn Moriarty. Evelyn told Carla that her cousin Junior Laemmle had passed away from a stroke. Carla said:

It was a strange coincidence that Junior passed away September 24, exactly 40 years to the day of his father's death. What I remember, personally, about Junior was a day when he came over to our bungalow at Universal. It was a beautiful day. We had walked down behind our bungalow where there was a rather uncultivated ravine. I saw that he needed someone to talk to. He was excited but concerned about not disappointing his father. This was not long before he became general manager at Universal. I have a copy of a letter that Junior wrote to his father around that time.

The letter was dated February 2, 1929. It reads as follows:

Dear Papa,
 Soon I will be twenty-one. Mere words lack the power of expression in allowing me to explain how much I appreciate your marvelous guidance in molding me from boy to man...My greatest ambition and aim in this world is to make your task easier by giving forth my life to further and carry on the monument which you have built through a life's work. Therefore I pledge myself to follow your slogan "It Can Be Done"... As the years roll on my wish is that people say there is a semblance of Carl, Sr. in Carl, Jr. In honor, ethics and ability.
 Your grateful and Loving Son, Junior.

The enthusiasm of youth met the harsh truth of reality when Carl, Jr. was forced into an early retirement by severe health problems. He had developed multiple sclerosis, a debilitating illness. Even the most advanced treatment could offer little real relief and no cure. His condition worsened after 1959. It was later learned that the "true love" of Junior Laemmle's life was the former Olympic swimmer and part-time actress, Eleanor Holm (*Tarzan's Revenge*, 1938), who passed away in Miami, Florida, January 31, 2004 at the age of 90. Junior will forever be remembered as the producer of *All Quiet on the Western Front*, but mostly he is revered for his contributions to the horror film genre.

It was also in 1979 that the Lane Magazine and Book Company listed *The Sea of Cortez* as out of print after 10 editions. Carla would spend the next 15 years trying to find a new publisher.

The 1980s were definitively a time of change for Carla Laemmle. She writes:

> When Ray came into my life everything changed for me. He was my Svengali. When Ray died it just about killed me, literally! I know from personal experience how very difficult and traumatic change can be. Change is one of the hardest things to accept in life. We want things to remain the same. But life is motion, and motion is change. And that's the way it is. It is my belief that we're all born into this world with a ledger of good and bad karma, which we have to pay up, but hopefully learn something from the experience so as not to repeat it again and again. Life is a school. Sometimes I think I just got out of kindergarten, if that much.

In July 1981, Carla was informed of yet another family death—her cousin, and famed movie director, William Wyler passed away at his Beverly Hills home at the age of 79.[1] Carla remembered:

> I knew my cousin, Willie Wyler in the early days at Universal. He was a very sweet man. He became an assistant director to my half-brother, Edward Laemmle. Of course Willie became a landmark movie director in Hollywood. Willie's "brother," Robert Wyler was also working in Hollywood as an assistant director. They were both very intelligent and caring people.[2]

Carla wrote for this book regarding her family:

> As the years go by, I realize that I am the only one left from the second generation of Laemmles on my Uncle Carl's side. I feel like my dear mother. She spent years researching the other side of the family. I know now, how

At Dios Dorados, the home of Carl Laemmle (1930) (seated to far left) William Beaudine, William Wyler. (on swing) Margaret Sullavan (behind her) Isadore Bernstein, Robert Wyler, Carla Laemmle, Julius Bernheim, Inga Bernheim, Maurice Fleckles, (standing to the side of Mr. Fleckles is) Alfred Stern and Mr. Fleckles' wife Anna (Stern). (seated in front of them are) Ernst Laemmle and Paul Kohner. (seated on ground from left) Henry Henigson, Jeanette Loff, and Carl Laemmle, Jr.

she must have felt being virtually the last survivor in her family with the exception of a few ancestors who wrote to her, none of whom she ever knew. All families live through triumphs and tragedies. We've all had our share. Other members of the Laemmle family were Walter and Ernst Laemmle. They were sons of Carl's brother Siegfried. Both of them had worked at Universal as assistant directors. Ernst was a successful movie director in the 1920s. He passed away in 1950. His wife, Nina, later won acclaim as the executive story producer of the highly successful TV series, *Marcus Welby, M.D.*

Walter Laemmle immigrated to America in 1927. He wasn't in the movie business. He was more like his father, Siegfried, and was interested in dealing art and antiques. He opened an antique store on La Cienega Boulevard in

West Hollywood and was the proprietor for many years. He nor his wife, Connie, were not connected to the movie industry. Walter Laemmle passed away in 1997.

Julius Bernheim was my second cousin. He was born in Germany. After Irving Thalberg left Universal in 1923, Julius was General Manager of Universal in 1924. Julius' son, Ronald, got in touch with me the past several years. It was great to see him after so many years. He was just a boy when I last saw him. Sadly, Julius' wife, Inge, was 26 when she died. Julius was 46 when his 26-year-old wife passed away. I was happy to see Ron again and meet his lovely wife, Lynn, for my 95th birthday. I was informed that Julius Bernheim passed away Wednesday, December 2, 1970.

There also were Richard and Eleanor Laemmle, my first cousins. I knew this would be not an easy assignment. It brings back painful memories of a time long past in the lives of Richard and Eleanor, and of my own along the way. They were brother and sister, the children of my Uncle Louis and Aunt Frieda Laemmle.

They say the past is dead, but not the emotions we experienced. Memories can trigger emotions. My memories merge the past into the present. The reason that some of the past is still painful is that nothing can be changed. The past is not a play that can be rewritten.

As in the immortal words of Omar Khayyam, "The Moving Finger, writes and having Writ, moves on; nor all your Piety nor Wit shall lure it back to cancel half a Line, Nor all your tears wash out a Word of it."

Be it a Cruel Fate or Karma, neither Richard nor Eleanor could escape their ill-starred destinies. The die was cast; both doomed to develop the insidious and devastating disorder of schizophrenia. It is a world of delusions, nonexistent voices, and hallucinations. The disease was so memorably enacted in the riveting 2001 Academy Award winning movie, *A Beautiful Mind*, based on the true story of the brilliant mathematician, John Nash.

In the cases of Richard and Eleanor, I believe the onset of the disorder began in their mid to late teens. They were both born in Chicago and I didn't see much of them in those very early days in Chicago. My earliest recollection of Richard did take place in Chicago. Richard was a mischievous little boy. One fourth of July, he set off some firecrackers in one of the dresser drawers of the posh Blackstone Hotel where the family was briefly staying.

Eleanor was a few years younger than Richard. She was a very pretty child with a somewhat pixie-like quality, and of course, that winning Laemmle smile. Both Richard and Eleanor were exceptionally well educated. Richard had an amazing mind, an extraordinary memory and an astonishing vocabulary. He had the potential for a successful and productive life.

My Uncle Louis Laemmle (father of Richard and Eleanor) moved his family from Chicago to Los Angeles during the early 1930s. Richard eventually worked at Universal as a scriptwriter, producer, director and film editor in the 1930s and 40s. For reasons I could only guess, he either quit or got fired. Richard, it seems, was not cut out for a structured lifestyle.

Eleanor matured into an attractive young woman with a nice personality. She found herself an excellent job as a secretary to a company executive. Life was good. At some point in time, Eleanor got married and had a child, a daughter, Peppi. Her family, as I remember, was not happy about her marriage. However, the marriage was rather short lived, possibly due to a combination of things, first among them, Eleanor's changing behavior pattern.

I have no memory as to who cared for Eleanor's child in those early days. When Peppi got older, my cousin Carol Bergerman, took over raising of the girl. Carol loved to take charge. Sometimes she overdid it. When Eleanor's daughter was grown, she packed her bags one day and just took off. We learned later that she got married. When Peppi contacted Eleanor by phone,

Edward Laemmle and Peppi Heller's wedding, April 8, 1923 in Los Angeles. Richard and Eleanor Laemmle (seated forefront), children of Louis Laemmle and Frieda Heller Laemmle that Carla kept touch with during their lives. Carl Laemmle (pictured at right of photo at head of table),

she told her mother that she didn't want to go back to Carol. She wanted to have her own family and lead her own life.

When Rosabelle died she left Peppi a $5000.00 bequest. Stanley was never able to locate her. We will never know what her destiny was or might have been. Richard was drafted into the Army during World War II. His weird behavior convinced the Army that he was not the most ideal material. After a period of time, he was given an Honorable Discharge and a small pension. It would later prove a Godsend as it was to become his only source of income.

There came a time when Richard's hallucinations and bizarre behavior had reached the point that his family had him committed to Camarillo Mental Hospital up the coast. He was there for about two years, I believe, but the medication they had then was not as effective as that which they give now. He managed to escape a couple of times and hitchhike back to L.A., but was always caught and sent back.

When Richard was finally released he lived briefly in an inexpensive hotel in Hollywood. But he couldn't afford it on a permanent basis. His father was long deceased by this time and the family had turned their backs on him. His choices became very limited. He bought an aged Cadillac that still had some mileage left and thereupon embarked upon an uncertain, unconventional lifestyle, a way of life he was to follow for the rest of his life. It was for him, his personal "declaration of independence, for life, liberty, and the pursuit of happiness."

His ever growing family of stray dogs he picked up filled his need for companionship. He was adamant in his refusal to spay any of them. It was their inherent right to mate and give birth. And that they did! It was dogs and man huddled together, living, sleeping and surviving in the limited space of his old Cadillac home on wheels, ever on the move to new locations and areas off the beaten path. It was a life of constant vigil, ever on guard against running into trouble with the law. It was difficult to avoid. In fact, Richard was arrested on a number of occasions. He spent some jail time on charges of cruelty to animals, a charge he would vehemently deny and vigorously argue in court. He learned a lot about legal matters acting as his own attorney. Despite the downside and the many difficulties attendant to his unorthodox lifestyle, Richard kept his faith and seldom let it dampen his resilient joi de vivre. From time to time Richard would show up at my house unannounced with his family of dogs in tow. Of course, I knew he would be hungry and thus, I always fixed he and his dogs something to eat.

There is no argument that Richard could try ones patience to the utmost, say, half-an-hour. It could be a true test of self-control. For Christmas in 1983, I sent him the following that I wrote myself:

To Richard, "The Royal Vagabundo"

The Sun shines on you,
Flowers bloom for you
Birds sing their songs for you,
For this is your Domain
Your way is off the beaten track,
Where there is no way,
You make one,
Whatever Heaven may bestow
in unexpected blessings,
you joyfully share with your
"Chosen Family", Those abiding
with you of another Kingdom.
In the eyes of men you may
Appear a poor eccentric,
In the eyes of your worshipful
subjects you are omniscient.

The Sun shines on you
Flowers bloom for you
Birds sing their songs to you.
It is your Domain,
And <u>You</u> are <u>King</u> !
Carla…

    I continued to correspond with Richard and sent him a small check from time to time. As his 72nd birthday was approaching [Saturday] April 20, 1985, I sent him a birthday card along with a check in care of his post office box in Pioneer Town, California. Sadly, he never had a chance to cash it. He was found dead outside of his parked car [Thursday] March 14, 1985 in San Bernardino, California. His 21 dogs, mostly puppies, were packed inside the car. I tried my best to find homes for the dogs.
    I was notified about all of this by the Public Administrator's Office in Riverside, California. They

had found my letter and check to Richard which was returned to me. They sent me another check at a later date for $237.21, the heir's share of Richard's estate. It was all pretty heartbreaking.

The nonconformist that Richard was, he made his life meaningful and equally important in the overall scheme of things. I've realized that the 50 odd letters to me from Richard are his only legacy. All you can ever know about Richard is to be found in these letters. They reveal Richard as the indomitable spirit that he was, the "Can do" kid ever striving for the unattainable. Shalom.

Eleanor's life likewise had a tragic ending. As she grew older, her schizophrenia worsened. She heard voices plotting against her. She had become more and more paranoid. Eleanor placed strips of aluminum foil around her windows. Although on strict doctor's medication, she was negligent in taking it. She was found dead after some days in her hotel room in the old St. Francis Hotel in Hollywood. Eleanor had lived there with her pet dog.

This unfortunate situation happened before Ray's passing. My cousins, Carol Bergerman and Carl Laemmle Junior, paid for Eleanor's burial. It was so sad. Her casket contained a body bag. She was buried at The Home of Peace Cemetery. Except for the Rabbi, who officiated at the brief service Carol and I were the only ones there.

During the mid-to-late 1980s, life for Carla Laemmle was filled with pleasant and meaningful days of travel. After returning from a trip to Egypt, Carla learned that her good friend Jimmy Dietrich had passed away. She wrote a letter to her friend violinist Lawrence Sommers letting him know of the passing of their mutual friend Jimmy Dietrich. Carla was happy to share the response that she received from Lawrence Sommers, written by him, from his home in Mountainhome, Pennsylvania, March 2, 1985:

Dear Carla,
How nice of you to write. After learning of Jimmy's [Dietrich] passing I was sorrowfully reminded that, with dear Helen in a coma, you were the only remaining

Alas, they meet again! Carla on the road with Lawrence Sommers (1988).

member of the "Dietrich Group" I knew of, and had no idea how to get in touch with you. To go back: I was in the habit of phoning Jimmy and Helen from time to time, and the last time I talked with Jimmy he told me that you danced at a function, and were as vital and entrancing as ever. He promised to send your address—never did!

Meanwhile, I wrote about Jimmy to a friend, Maria Moody, who lives in Van Nuys. She's a painter, amateur musician, and is into occult doings—astrology, etc. Perhaps you know her. At any rate, she took it upon herself to call Jimmy, as she is the gregarious type, and learned he was in the hospital following an accident, and was to be operated upon the very next day, an operation he did not survive. However, it was some weeks before she wrote me of this, and she did not know of his death. I immediately called, and it was then that I learned from Jacques that "Jimmy had passed on." I asked Jacques for your address, and he promised to send it on, but you beat him to it!

You, along with the Dietrichs and a few others, were well-remembered participants in a very exciting slice of my life, and I felt that by getting in touch with you I could retain some of the excitement and color of that bygone time. So many are gone, or no longer to be found. A few years ago I was out there, and soon became aware of the fact that many old friends simply could not be located. Virginia Marshall was one. She, Helen and I had a concert trio, remember? Another was Suzanne Torres, the mother-in-law of Nico Charisse. After Cyd quit Nico for greener fields he married Zita Torres. I thought it would be a cinch to locate them, but no such luck. Do you know what happened to the Charisses? Perhaps back in France, as they were all French. Some evidently had unlisted phones, and in one case the home of friends in West L.A. had been bulldozed to make way for a Freeway. So it went. I asked about you when I saw Helen, but it seems you were in the midst of personal difficulties at the time—in short, no time to "intrude," So it went.

My one definite contact out there is Henry Roth, a violinist and critic whom I knew as a 16-year old. He has become a prestigious writer—several books—and is music critic for the B'nai B'rith *Messenger*, and has gifted me with a subscription for at least eight to 10 years. Both Henry and his wife Esther have visited here with us numerous times, and we correspond all the time... I still remember your enchanting dancing, and the endearing way you plied *Her Majesty the Prince* with wine...Also the appearance with Helen and me at the Chinese Festivals. Your esteemed friend Ray Cannon is also remembered—an extremely talented and colorful personality.

Also remembered is your dear mother, who, in a quiet way, exhibited such unmistakable gentility. As the old song goes—"those were the days, my friend; we thought they'd never end..."

I imagine you may have gleaned a few details of my own life from Jimmy and Helen. After the war, during which I spent four years in the army, from private to captain, I toured musically with the two groups—the

Carla Laemmle as Princess Quan Mui Mai in the play *Her Majesty the Prince* (1936).

Dorelle Trio, and the N.Y. Art Quartette, and also did some sole appearances, mostly for colleges and cultural clubs.

In 1950 I married Gertrude Hopkins, a nationally known harpist, and we are still together. A wonderful person and a *real* person in every sense of the word. Perhaps some day you'll get to meet her. We have done a lot of travel, and she has done so much to "pull my life together. If I do say so, there were quite a few aspects of superficiality in my Hollywood period, and I'm sure you must have noticed that. A dead-end street, so to speak. If there is to be blame, let it be my own immaturity and inexperience, which confused glitter with substance.

And then you've no doubt heard how I became the editor of a highly successful *Astrology Magazine* for 19 years. Then I found I could not take it any more—simply written out. Meanwhile had turned out a book for the meretricious Jeane Dixon, an episode that ended in my being victorious over her obvious effort to shut me out of the profits. A long and devious story.

I've rambled on, but did so, dear Carla, on the assumption that you actually knew little of the real ME. For example, why live here, in these Poconos? It began in 1765, when my mother's ancestor's (Welsh) settled in this forested region. In 1832 my father's grandfather (German) arrived in the same locality. During this century the Poconos gradually became a popular resort area—my mother was the owner of two hotels—and today it is really humming with activity. For instance, our little town is far from bucolic—five restaurants, six service stations, a medical center, drug store, supermarket, two banks and numerous shops and establishments that cater "mostly to the tourist trade." Oh, yes. We also have the famous Pocono Playhouse, a summer theater. So you see it is not exactly the boondocks.

We live in a comfortable house on an acre of ground, surrounded by woodlands. We settled here quite by accident. Gertrude is a New Yorker (Long Island) and country living didn't appeal at first, but now she seems to like the leisurely pace and pleasant surroundings. And now spring is almost here, and then Pocono foliage really takes off and I'll be busy with my gardening. No music now, other than listening.

So it goes, dear Carla. Now that I've found out your whereabouts let us keep in touch. Old friends are few and far between these days. How do I look? Well, a little heavier, have most of my hair, which is white, have no discernable health problems, and live life with gusto....

With nostalgic affection, Lawrence.

Carla recalled that Lawrence Sommers had lived in Los Angeles with his first wife Ann, during the early days until her unfortunate death around the start of World War II. He moved east where he remarried and lived in Mountainhome, Pennsylvania for many years. Then his second wife, Gertrude passed away. Carla's memories of Lawrence Sommers are fond ones. She made a trip to see Lawrence Sommers at his home in Mountainhome, Pennsylvania in the fall of 1988. Lawrence met her at the airport in Newark, New Jersey. Carla recalled:

We had a fabulous time. I met some of his friends and had some delectable dinners. Back in the earlier days, Lawrence had written some lovely songs for Ray's play, *Her Majesty the Prince*..."Little Blue Pigeon" and "La Danse DE LA PRINCESSE, Quan Mui Mai." Lawrence had written *A Legend of Old China*. It grabbed the attention of the Writer's Guild [May, 1940]. He was a most talented violinist, but I think that he should have made more of his writing. He was really the only friend from the old days that I had left. He wanted to do some traveling at this time in his life, after his second wife passed away. He asked if I would accompany him.

We agreed on our chosen journeys and had an amazing time. We went on two trips soon after I arrived. The first was driving across the States from Mountainhome, Pennsylvania out to California. We went up through California to Montreal, Canada. The fall of the year was the best time to go. The scenery was breathtaking! For the second trip we drove through upstate New York. We were in Connecticut where I revisited my mother's heritage. There, I also visited the famed Loomis Institute. The trip went well. Lawrence and I were great friends. I know that he "wanted it to be more than that, but I'll suffice to say that he got over it. We had a lot of respect for one another. Lawrence accepted that we were just good friends. We laughed a lot! Lawrence had quite a sense of

> humor. I remember back in 1936 when Lawrence had an operation on his nose. Afterward, I thought that he had a profile like John Barrymore!
>
> After the second trip, Lawrence asked me if I would like to go on a European tour trip as a special treat all at his expense. I was thrilled of course and began planning for it. Tickets were purchased and all arrangements made when suddenly I got very sick and had to cancel the trip the day before I was to leave. It was heartbreak. The doctor's diagnosis was tuberculosis. I spent practically a whole year recovering from it! I do not know where I could have contracted it unless it happened during my previous travels to China, Japan and Egypt.

Carla's trip to Pennsylvania would be the last time that she and Lawrence Sommers would see each other in person, however they continued a written correspondence until 1992. Carla, remembers Lawrence being extremely attentive, as well as humorous, clever and a really brilliant writer. His letters display those qualities. Carla would learn from his letters that he had cancer. Lawrence Sommers passed away in Philadelphia, Pennsylvania, on Sunday, October 11, 1992.

For Carla Laemmle the 1990s ran the gamut of emotions. Before the end of the decade, Carla would turn 90 years of age. In retrospect, Carla said:

> I saw some of my long-lived dreams come true. They were eventful and exciting times. Some were also sorrowful.

As time moves on, Carla keeps herself busy and is still a fan of movies. *Babe* was an instant favorite. "I really love that movie. It has such heart!"

In the autumn of 1994, Carla's 64-year-old cousin Carol Bergerman had passed away. Carla remembered:

> Carol's sudden and tragic death was a great shock to me. I was deeply saddened too, not only for myself, but for her 91–year-old father, Stanley Bergerman as well. Carol and I had been out of touch for too long. And the way

Grandpapa Carl with his only granddaughter, Carol. Beverly Hills, Ca. 1938.

I heard about Carol's death was through a neighbor of mine who read it in the local obituaries of the newspaper. I immediately phoned Stanley. He first apologized and then went on to say that everything had happened so suddenly. Carol's stepmother, Fay Bergerman, took the phone and further explained that she and Stanley had booked a cruise and were literally walking out the door to go on vacation when the telephone rang [Monday, November 28, 1994]. It was the Los Angeles Authorities informing Stanley of his daughter's death. It had to be difficult for Stanley to have survived his daughter. No parent would want this to happen.

Thursday December 1, 1994, Carole Laemmle Bergerman was laid to rest at the Laemmle Family Room, in the mausoleum at the Home of Peace Memorial Park in Whittier, California. She was the sixth family member to be interred there.

Experiencing the death of a loved one during the holiday season knows that December can be a sad and depressing time. Carla was not looking forward to the 1994 holiday season. Carole Bergerman's death occurred four days after Thanksgiving.

Publishing would again affect Carla's life when, seventeen years after Ray Cannon's death, Carla would discover he was not forgotten.

> Out of the blue, an independent publisher, Mike Bales, came to see me with an interest in publishing a biographical book on Ray and his writings. I was elated, of course! It was the answer to my dreams. I thought that Santa Claus had really come! We signed an agreement and I turned all of Ray's material over to Mike Bales, who in turn, turned it over to Gene Kira.

Carla collaborated with Gene Kira for over four years before her dream was realized. The beautiful and elegant *The Unforgettable Sea of Cortez* (July, 1999) gave new meaning to Carla Laemmle's life.

But the book was not the only adventure awaiting Carla in 1995. After meeting Mike Bales, Carla met yet another enterprising and caring individual by the name of Forrest J Ackerman, known to baby boomer monster kids as Uncle Forry, 4SJ, or just plain ol' Forry. When Mr. Ackerman, a native of Los Angeles, was a youngster, he wrote letters to studio head Carl Laemmle critiquing the horror movies released by Universal.

Many, many years later, Forry and Carl's niece Carla met through mutual friends at an informal showing of 1931's *Dracula*. Forry had no idea that he was sitting in the same room with someone who had actually been in the movie—Carla Laemmle. Everyone was in on the joke and

Carla with her good friend Forrest J Ackerman (1995).

sworn to secrecy and agreed to just play along. Carla used an alias when she and Forry were introduced earlier in the evening...

> Suddenly, the movie begins. The music from "Swan Lake" begins to play...the opening credits appear... The credits fade to a horse drawn coach riding along. The next scene shows the passengers aboard the coach...then a woman's voice...suddenly Forry asks if his hosts had "surroundsound." Carla was speaking her lines in sync to her character on the screen. Forry says, "That was good. Bravo ! Have you ever thought about being in the movies?" Carla answered Forry by saying, "Thank you... and yes...I was in the movies and...that was me!

Carla remembered later that Forry really hadn't the foggiest idea who she was. Carla became quite fond of Forry. Forry has shared 10 of 12 birthdays with Carla and this writer before he passed away December 4, 2008..

Forry is a very charming and caring person. Although Bela Lugosi passed away many years ago and was much older than myself, it wasn't until that evening when I learned that I shared the same birthday with Bela Lugosi, but he was born October 20, 1882.

Carla continued:

Not long after we met, Forry invited me to one of his conventions. It was called Son of Famous Monsters of Filmland, Horror, Sci-Fi and Fantasy World Convention. Ironically, it took place at the Universal-Sheraton Hotel here in Los Angeles. When I lived at Universal City, the area where the Hotel now stands was prairie land. Nonetheless, I felt a type of homecoming as I enjoyed being a participant in a special awards dinner one evening. I also participated by signing my autograph for many people of all ages. I signed books, photos and movie posters. I felt as though I was giving good to people. It is unfortunate what Forry endured later through the courts. Apparently, after years of being the editor of his own magazine [*Famous Monsters of Filmland* 1958-1995], another party would join causing Forry to later file charges of plagiarism against the individual. It went on for years! I am happy that it is all past for Forry now. He attended some of my birthday celebrations in the past several years. The most memorable time was when Forry came to my home for my birthday in 2003 and 2005. It was really courageous of him to come to my party in 2005. He had just had brain surgery. In time he made a full recovery. Forry Ackerman is a lovely man. He lives about 15 minutes away from me. I continue to see him on occasion. He is such a wealth of information. And he sings to me on occasion. He is, what I am not, a good singer. I did tell Forry about the song that I wrote and had copyrighted.[3]

The German Black Forest Inn in Santa Monica, California (1997). (from left to right) Carla Laemmle, Michal Kerestes, Gabriele Bayer, Fay Bergerman, Udo Bayer and Stanley Bergerman.

In 1996, after learning of the Carl Laemmle/Laupheim Museum Project in Laupheim Württemberg, Germany, Carla said, "Udo Bayer knows more about Carl Laemmle's life in Germany than any one person."

Carla was intrigued by the idea of the museum and the three Carl Laemmle rooms that were eventually installed and dedicated. The museum has helped her learn more about the homeland of her uncle and her father.

Stanley Bergerman began corresponding with Udo Bayer and the City of Laupheim, Germany in the spring of 1995. The Mayor of Laupheim wrote to Mr. Bergerman on two occasions regarding appreciation of gifts that Stanley had sent in memory of Carl Laemmle to Laupheim for the expansion of their museum,.

The summer of 1997 Udo Bayer and his wife, Gabriele (also known as Gabi) made a trip to Los Angeles to meet Stanley Bergerman and Carla Laemmle.

While in California, the Bayers also met Carl Laemmle Junior's close friend, Evelyn Moriarty, who lived in North Hollywood. Carla and the Bayers visited the USC Archive Department, where they found extensive documentation regarding Carl Laemmle and Universal Pictures. The

Carla Laemmle with Ernest Schall (standing) and Udo Bayer at the Laupheim, Germany Jewish Cemetery (August 20, 1997).

Bayers also got to meet Forrest J Ackerman at his Glendower Avenue home, which was fondly known to fans as the Son of Ackermansion. Carla signed Forry's guestbook and remarked: "His Museum/Home is amazing!" Later everyone met at the German Black Forest Inn in Santa Monica for dinner. Attending the dinner were Stanley and Fay Bergerman, Carla Laemmle, Michal Kerestes, who is Carla's attorney and friend, and Udo and Gabriele Bayer. The Bayers stayed in America for two weeks. Carla thoroughly enjoyed their visit and found Udo and his wife, an utterly charming couple.

Monday, August 18, 1997, following the Bayer's visit to America, Carla Laemmle and Michal Kerestes found themselves aboard a European airline enroute to Laupheim, Germany. Carla wrote:

> At this point in time, I figure it's now or never. And in the meantime, before we leave on the trip, I am scheduled to be a guest at the 100th Anniversary of the book *Dracula*

hosted by my friend, David Skal. Then, after our return to L.A., I was invited as a guest to the Cinecon Conference-Film Festival. It seemed like an awful big place. I hoped that I could survive.

She did. The trip to Germany was a dream come true for Carla. From a journal, Carla wrote:

> I wonder about all these people on the plane, each with their own destinations and stories. I don't think any of them can top mine! Who would have dreamed that I would be making this fabulous trip to Germany at this point of my life. It is like a fairy tale. How happy my parents would be. I hope Uncle Carl, Junior and Rosabelle are smiling.

Carla and Michal were houseguests of the Bayer's and their two teenaged children, Isabel and Mirko. Carla was moved by the fact that she and Isabel shared her middle name. She and Michal visited the town of Ulm, where Albert Einstein was born. There they saw the stupendous 13th-century cathederal. They would gaze at many medieval castles and churches before their departure. The Bayers also took Carla and Michal on a "delightful boat ride on the Danube." One of their visits was to see the "Carl Laemmle Gymnasium." Carla wrote of the trip:

> Michal and I were treated like royalty. My heart was so full, I cried when we had to say goodbye.

Carla and Michal left Germany on August 28, 1997.

The trip to Laupheim was a great testimonial to the Laemmle family memory. Even before the trip, helping to preserve the memory and legacy of "Uncle Carl" was important to Carla. At one point Laemmle was a considered candidate for a Nobel prize. But it never happened. To this day Carla keeps learning more about the history of her family's native Laupheim and its people.

Sadly, Carla received a heartbreaking telephone call from Fay Bergerman July 13, 1998 informing her that Stanley Bergerman had passed away that morning. Carla said,

That was a knockout blow! His friendship meant so much to me. He was the closest thing to "family" that I had. Now there are none. It will be very hard for Fay to adjust to life without Stanley. They were so close.

Stanley Bergerman was interred at Hillside Memorial Park located in the Culver City area of Los Angeles.

In March 1998, Carla was invited back to Laupheim, Germany to appear on German television with the Honorable Mayor of Laupheim, Otmar Schick. She and Michal Kerestes once again took off for Europe. For this weeklong trip the Mayor arranged to have his guests stay in a hotel.

The trip was all "very delightful." The first couple of days were spent shopping and seeing the countryside. Later, Carla had a videotaped interview with the Mayor, Otmar Schick. After the interview Udo Bayer had arranged for Carla to meet with students for a question and answer session. Carla writes,

> In as much as I was wearing my beautiful Chinese coat that I got in Hong Kong, and a stage was set up behind me. I felt the urge to get up on the stage and perform a little Chinese dance. I asked first if they'd like to see it. Well of course! So I got up there and did it! That was a complete joy.

The television show in which Carla appeared was similar to the American *What's My Line*. Carla was the panelist and the contestants had to guess her identity. The outcome was that someone did guess correctly. Carla was so loved by the citizens of Laupheim that she had become a star.

Carla revisited the museum project to find that the interior construction was progressing. Local German newspaper photographers took many shots the day that Carla, Udo Bayer and Ernst Schall visited the Laupheim cemetery. Carla and Michal returned to Los Angeles, Wednesday, March 18, 1998.

In the 70 years since Carl Laemmle had been president at Universal City there have been a number of new managements since being sold to Standard Capital in 1936:

• 1946, Universal merged with International Pictures to become Universal-International Pictures until a merger with Decca Records in 1952.
• 1959, the Music Corporation of America (MCA) acquired Decca Records and Universal.
• 1990, the Matsushita Electric Industrial Company purchased MCA.
• 1995, The Seagrams Company purchased control of MCA and Universal. The establishment was renamed Universal Studios.
• 1998, Universal purchased the USA Network.
• 2000, Universal merged with a French global media company called Vivendi Media Group and became known as Vivendi/Universal, which acquired Seagrams entertainment holdings.
• April 2004, Vivendi/Universal was purchased by and merged with the National Broadcasting Company. The conglomerate is currently known as NBC/Universal.

Tuesday, March 15, 2005 was the 90th anniversary of the opening of Universal Pictures. It was just another day at the studio, no fanfare, no celebration.

Three months after Carla's third trip to Germany, she celebrated her 90th birthday with this writer, his mother Faye Atkins and his brother Dean. All had a gala time.

Carla was also learning of other family members from the Mrs. Carl Laemmle side—the Stern family. She met with them in 1999, before she left on her last trip to Germany. She and three members of the Stern family had dinner at a Beverly Hills restaurant. Carla was pleased to find additional relations.

Carla's Uncle Carl had no direct connections to the Laemmle Theatres operating in Southern California. The owners were Max Laemmle and his brother Kurt, who were sons of Carla's Uncle Siegfried. This made Max, Carla's first cousin.

Max Laemmle opened his first movie theater (The Los Feliz) in 1940, a year after Carl Laemmle had passed away. Max's son Robert Laemmle eventually took over the business after his father's death. Robert and his son, Greg continued to run the family chain of theatres. Kurt Laemmle passed away in 1994 at the age of 85.

July 20, 1999. Carla Laemmle and this writer boarded an aircraft bound for Europe. It turned out to be life-changing for both of us. The destination was the province of Baden Württemberg, Laupheim, Germany. We were guests of the Honorable Mayor Otmar Schick and houseguests of Dr. and Mrs. Udo Bayer. Carla, in a hushed voice said, "We're moving!" as the plane began to taxi down the runway. The airplane's engines roared as the plane began rising from the ground of Southern California. Carla leaned back in her seat and said in a whispered tone, "Take off!" We were at last on our way to our European adventure.

When the plane leveled off Carla turned to her future biographer and smiled, "I love you! We're really going to Germany together!"

Carla was the last passenger to finish eating dinner that evening. In fact, she was always the last to finish eating anywhere on the trip. I asked jokingly if taking one's time eating was the secret to her longevity? She said with half a nod, "I really don't know but I've always been a slow eater." We giggled.

Great relief was felt when Flight 061 arrived at Charles DeGaulle airport the morning of July 22, 1999. The flight had taken 11 hours. At the age of 89, Carla was taking it all in stride. However, we had to move quickly to catch the connecting flight to Stüttgart, Germany. With our arrival in Stüttgart, we were surprised to be greeted by Carla's New York cousin and her husband; Ruth and Eddie Regis, who had arrived on a separate flight. Carla had learned of her long lost cousin Ruth Friedland Regis from Udo Bayer in early 1998. This was their very first meeting.

Gabriele Bayer, better known as Gabi, soon arrived to meet us. Our gracious and beautiful hostess and chauffeur drove the 60-mile trip to Laupheim. We had our fair share of conversation. Ruth reminisced about her many European childhood memories and of her place on the Laemmle family tree. Ruth and Carla were third cousins.

Ruth was born in Biberach, Germany and lived in Laupheim with her family until 1933. The family relocated to Paris because of the increasing anti-Semitism in Germany. She came to the United States in 1939—sponsored by Carl Laemmle. Her parents joined her in 1940. Mrs. Regis lost two aunts to the Holocaust.

For over 50 years, Ruth and her husband, Eddie Regis made their home in New York. By the time that Udo Bayer caught up with them they were residents of Kingsbridge Heights. The Regis' first trip to Laupheim was a reunion of 46 former Jewish residents of Laupheim, who had been invited back as a goodwill gesture by the German government.

Carla's second cousin, the late, Ruth Friedland Regis and her late husband, Eddie Regis with Carla and the author enroute to the dedication ceremonies at the Carl Laemmle Gymnasium. (July 24, 1999).

The countryside of South Central Germany (Bavaria) appeared similar to that of the Southern United States, particularly Tennessee, although the German countryside is much larger. The scenery was beautiful!

Entering the immaculate town of Laupheim, the speed limit suddenly changes to a mere crawl. There is an interesting blend of modernization and old European charm in many of the town structures.

We were all luncheon guests at the hotel restaurant Zum Wyse. There we were greeted by our host, Dr. Udo Bayer and his associate Dr. Anna-Ruth Löwenbrück, both co-curators at the Laupheim museum (SchloBGroBlaupheim Museum zur Geschichte von Christen & Juden). The Regis' would be staying at the hotel. After a delectable lunch, we were whisked away by our host to the museum.

The Laupheim museum was a magnificent structure with an important historical significance. The building was originally a castle that dates back to 1550 with additions later added to the right side in 1660 and the left side in 1750. Learning about Laupheim was fascinating. The first Jewish settlers arrived in 1730. By 1850 Laupheim was considered a Jewish community. Their Synagogue was erected in 1836. A memorial stone now marks the site of the Laupheim Synagogue and features a commemorative plaque naming the Laupheimers who lost their lives between 1938 and 1944. Toward the end of the museum tour, Mr. Roland Ray a reporter for the German newspaper *Schiväbische Zeitung*, greeted us. Mr. Ray interviewed both Carla and this writer separately.

The Laemmles of Laupheim were a German-Jewish family. Carl Laemmle was the tenth of 13 children born to Rebekkah and Julius Baruch Laemmle. Carl and the other siblings presumably were born at home, in a building that was erected in 1823.

On the first day of our nine-day tour, we visited the birthplace of Carl Laemmle, a building that Carla had first visited in 1997. The town baker and his family were residing in the house at the time of our visit. The second floor quarters are set up as an Inn or temporary apartment space. One has to obtain city permission to visit this establishment. It was cited as a town landmark by the City of Laupheim. The home is featured in many of Carl Laemmle's past visits to his homeland. It was dedicated with an outdoor plaque from the year 1987.

The people of Laupheim are humble and hospitable. We also visited neighboring towns such as Ulm (birthplace of Albert Einstein), Biberach, and Ochsenhausen. Another of the fascinating sites in Southern Germany is the cathedral in nearby Ulm. It has the highest church steeple in the world, 534 feet. Ulm an der Donau was dedicated in 1877. The cathedral took 500 years to complete. The festive day of the trip followed the dedication ceremonies of the new wing at the Carl Laemmle School. The entertainment was presented and choreographed by the young students of Laupheim. As the show started, we guests from the United States were introduced individually and asked to stand for acknowledgment. The students performed a variety of song, music and dance numbers during the three-hour program.

After the reception, Gabi suggested that we attend a coffee break at the exquisite Café Hermes. The Café was once the former home and birthplace of Friedrich Adler, a prominent sculptor and artist. We were met by women who were on the Board of the Laupheim Historical Society. Carla and Ruth were presented with honorary scrolls naming them as members of the society. Among those present was Liesel Adler of England, niece of the artist Friedrich Adler. The adorable Miss Adler was present on several occasions during our stay.

Once a 16th Century castle is now the Laupheim Museum in Baden Württemberg as it appears today

We also visited the cemetery in Laupheim (Jüdishischer Friedhof Laupheim), located in the town center on the Judenberg. There are 36 known Laemmle graves at the Jewish Cemetery in Laupheim. Carla's grandparents, Julius Baruch Laemmle and Rebekkah Laemmle, are buried there. Nine of the 13 Laemmle children are also interred there including Carl's sister Karoline, and her husband, Jakob Bernheim, the grandparents Ruth Regis. The Cemetery today stands as its own memorial to WWII and the holocaust. The grandparents of Karoline and Jakob Bernheim, are also buried in the Laupheim cemetery. Carl Laemmle, his brothers, Joseph, Louis, and Siegfried are buried in the United States.

There are approximately 1,000 preserved gravestones out of the 1,200 graves in the historical cemetery.

Records indicate that three trains bound for concentration camps left Laupheim during Hitler's regime. The last train carried 43 people, mostly parents and grandparents of townspeople, most of whom would never return. Friedrich Adler, who had designed a number of the gravestones placed at the Laupheim cemetery (including those of Julius and Rebekkah Laemmle), was aboard one of those trains. Mr. Adler died in Auschwitz in 1942, the same year the last family of Jews in Laupheim were deported. Today, there are no Jews living in Laupheim.

Miss Holderle's joy in photographing Carla! Carla loves the camera! And, the camera loves her! (Laupheim, Germany 1999).

During the last four days in Laupheim, we were invited to the home of Mr. and Mrs. Haffner for a fondue. The highlight of the evening came just after the table was cleared. The Haffners lit several candles and placed them about the table. Mr. Haffner commenced to tell a ghost story in their darkened dining room while iced desserts were served.

One morning Elisabeth Lincke, a woman from the Laupheim Historical Society, who Carla had met on her previous trips, arrived to show us the nearby village of Biberach. We would return to join the Mayor for German/Chinese cuisine, the most popular in Laupheim. Dinner that evening was spent at an outdoor cafe beside the Danube River.

Our last full day in Laupheim was spent visiting two castles. While walking down the steep hill at Waldburg castle, Carla taught this writer to memorize her opening line from the motion picture, *Dracula*. "Among the rugged peaks that frown down upon the Borgo Pass, are found crumbling castles of a bygone age." Carla said with her Laemmle smile, "You are going to know this by heart, before you go home!"

Proud Carla holds a copy of the recently published *The Unforgettable Sea of Cortez* as a gift to the Laupheim Museum, as a special on looker smiles alongside her (July 1999).

Later that afternoon while shopping in Laupheim, Carla spotted the Mayor near the newspaper office. She asked Gabi to stop so she could say her farewell. Mayor Schick was being photographed by a young lady who was amazed by Carla Laemmle. Gabi told us that the photographer, Uschi Holderle, had a photography studio just down the road and would like to take Carla there to photograph her. Carla said, "Her studio?... Now? Sure! I'll go!" Carla met up with Miss Holderle at her studio where she took several photographs of Carla. One of the pictures became a window display for the store before Christmas that year.

Our last dinner in Laupheim was spent at the famed Black Oxen Restaurant where Carl Laemmle ate his last European meal. The interior of the Restaurant was preserved in it's original splendor. We were told that the original floors were preserved for over three quarters of a century. The meal was simply delicious! Laupheim's German cuisine is prepared

Gary J. Svehla presents the first Laemmle Award to Carla Laemmle at Monster Rally.

lighter than other southern regions in Germany, probably because of a Swabia influence.

Our last morning, as we drove away from Laupheim, Gabi took us to the St. Georg church in nearby Ochsenhausen. This church has been referred by some townspeople as "the skeleton church." This church is simply breathtaking and is truthfully indescribable. The last photograph that was taken on the 17th roll of film was at the street sign that read "Carl Laemmle Street." Carla said, "I'm so glad we got to go to the street that was named after my uncle and took a picture there!" Ruth agreed. Eddie said, "It's a rather old looking sign."[4]

The experience of this nine-day trip did not stop there. It turned out, however to be an inspiring and remarkable 21-day trip in all. Nine additional days were spent back in Los Angeles at Carla's home... then three days at the Crystal City Hyatt in Virginia, near Washington DC, for the Monster Rally '99 Convention. Carla signs hundreds of autographs at events such as these. They are usually weekend long events held by varieties of film enthusiasts and/or editors of movie and celebrity publications. That particular weekend, the first annual Carl Laemmle Award Presentation took center stage. An impressive array of celebrities were on hand as Carla Laemmle was presented with the first award of the evening, a sculpture of Carl Laemmle designed by noted artist Henry Alverez. She accepted it in memory of her illustrious Uncle Carl. She loves appearing at each and every event that she is invited to.

Before the new millennium, Carla learned through Udo Bayer that she had a living relative from the fourth generation. Rosemary Hilb is the granddaughter of Carla's half-brother, Edward Laemmle. Having met her great-niece, Rosemary, Carla was soon to meet Rosemary's two young daughters as well. In addition to this great surprise, Udo Bayer had located in his search for surviving German immigrants who were sponsored by Carl Laemmle, Mrs. Ruth Henle Chernoff. Ruth came to America in 1938 at the age of 17, with her father Alwin Henle (now deceased). Ruth's grandfather was Moritz Henle, who composed Choral music at the Laupheim Synagogue. Ruth and Leonard Chernoff have been married since 1947. Carla was surprised to learn that the Chernoffs live just an hour away from her.

The new millennium brought with it another surprise to Carla Laemmle's life. She received a letter "out of the blue" from Stephen Gallagher, the grandson of Ray Cannon. Mr. Gallagher received the book, *The Unforgettable Sea of Cortez* from a relative as a gift. When Stephen read of Carla Laemmle in the book, he wrote to her. Carla was delighted to hear from him. They began corresponding and Stephen made the trip from his home in Missouri to visit Carla Laemmle for the first time in September 2000, shortly before her 91st birthday. Carla truly values all her newfound relationships. Prior to Stephen's arrival, Carla wrote the following in a letter to this writer in June 2000:

> I have never been able to feel Ray's presence. I have desired it so very much. I talk to him all the time and ask him to give me a sign but I have not been able to lift the veil that separates us. But I have no doubt that my love, our love, is a lasting bond that will bring us together again and again in whatever planes manifestation may be. I have always known he was far along on the Path and perhaps even halted the course to help me. I learned so much of goodness and beauty from him. Yesterday, as usual, I had the radio on and something they were playing inspired me to get up and dance with him. But it was much more than that. I had the urge to get

Ray's picture and dance with him! I held it before me as I—we—danced. Tears were just streaming down my face. It was truly a spiritual moment in time. I thought afterwards, what would anyone think of such a scene? But it seemed so natural to me and I was "not" 90 years old. I was "young" and expressing my love. Anyway, I know you will understand. As a matter of fact, I thought, what a heart-tugging scene it would make in a movie, and I was doing it in real life...

Carla was filmed for a television commercial in the summer of 2000. Her local Meals on Wheels organization and The PGA (Professional Golfer's Association) Productions photographed Carla at her home. Sharing the day's events, Carla wrote:

After we did that little filming this morning I realized how much I miss the professional life. I really do love it—every phase of it. You know how I liked to pose every chance I got, in those very early pictures! Maybe in the next life I'll pick up where I left off and really amount to something..."

Has Carla Laemmle forgotten something? She had achieved quite a reputable cult status by this time in her life and still receives an abundance of fan mail. In 1998, executives with Universal Home Video planned to re-released a series of their Classic Monsters Collection on DVD—the Bela Lugosi version of *Dracula* and the simultaneous Spanish version of 1931 was their first choice. David Skal (a personal friend of Carla) was hired to write and direct the added features that accompanied each release. David wrote a script for Carla for the documentary which was included with the premiere DVD release of *Dracula*. It was titled *The Road to Dracula*.

A Universal Studios film crew arrived at Carla Laemmle's home Halloween night, 1998. The film crew set up a backdrop in her living room. The ambiance came complete with candelabra and a gothic chair for her to sit in while she spoke every word of her script that she had memorized in only two days. Carla Laemmle was once again at her best. The DVD was released in retail stores throughout the United States on December 21, 1999.

"Forry" Ackerman, Carla Laemmle and the author celebrate Carla's 91st birthday at the Dresden Room (Los Angeles, October, 2000).

In a letter, dated September 17, 2000 to this writer, Carla wrote:

> I learned through my friend David Skal, that Universal Studios Home Video won the DiVi Award for Best Standard Release. That is quite an honor, isn't it? I am glad to have hosted, *The Road to Dracula* documentary.

In the same letter, Carla had other news.

> I have just completed a cameo in a movie called *The Vampire Hunter's Club*, a spoof on horror movies. The movie also features Forry Ackerman, David Skal, and actress, Mink Stole. they expect to show it at The Cult Theatre around October 20th! I play an "elderly" vampire in the movie with a couple of lines of dialogue. It was a lot of fun to do."

In early 2001, Carla Laemmle was 91 years of age and life for her during this time was peaceful. She continues to receive and answers all of her fan mail from all over the United States and internationally. She practices daily Ti Chi exercises and began studying the Kabbalah in April of 2001.[5]

In August 2001, Udo and Gabriele Bayer returned to the United States from Germany for a two week visit. Carla Laemmle was at the top of their visiting list. The Bayers and Carla had a festive week together. Before the couple left for Hawaii, they and Carla visited such places as the UCLA Archives and Universal Pictures. The Bayers and Carla visited Fay Bergerman, the widow of Stanley Bergerman and also Forry Ackerman. The Bayers' California visit wasn't complete without another visit with Evelyn Moriarty in her North Hollywood home.

Carla, like the rest of the world was devastated on Sept. 11, 2001. She wrote on October 11, 2001:

> I fear that America will never be the same again. How such a tragedy could be so successfully pulled off is beyond comprehension. Our highly rated Intelligence Agency really blew it. We found out how vulnerable we are. Our way of life will not be the same anymore, at least not until *all* the terrorists have been found and dealt with. In the meantime, we are living with the constant fear of what's next! It is not easy to try to live a normal life these days.

In the aftermath and fear that followed 911, Carla was most understanding when our traditional "double birthday celebration" did not take place in 2001. However, Father Time arrived, Saturday, October 20, 2001. Carla Laemmle turned 92. This was a day of observation for Carla. She is the last surviving second generation member of the Carl Laemmle family. She has lived longer than any of her family members.

In a letter of April 2002, Carla expressed her feelings after having composed a biographical piece for Udo Bayer and her relationship with Ray Cannon, with the following:

> ...I don't know how Udo intends to use the material. It centers so much on my relationship with Ray. He was, after all, a very great part of my life and now still it seems. The spiritual bond between us is a strong one, like a magnet. It will draw us together again in the eternity of things. I am sure of it. It is very difficult not to be caught up by the hypnotism of life. We fall under the spell of it,

obviously to the impermanence of it all on this earthly plane of existence. Round and round, desire brings us back. It is all so bittersweet.

The friendship that has developed between the Bayer family and Carla has greatly enriched her life. They have all individually become most dear to her as have the friendly people of Laupheim and their former Mayor. "Otmar Schick was a wonderful Mayor." She feels fortunate and blessed in these latter years of her life.

The "double birthday celebration" for the year 2002, was memorable for Carla's 93rd birthday. In addition to all of the festivities there was a lunch with Forry Ackerman and our annual visit with Carla's friend, Evelyn Moriarty, who had recently become a resident of the Motion Picture and Television Hospital. We continued to visit Evelyn there annually. (Sadly, Evelyn Moriarty passed away May 21, 2008. She was interred at Westwood Cemetery, near the crypt of her friend Marilyn Monroe, for whom she was Marilyn's lively stand-in for the last three years of the star's life.) Carla said of her good friend Evelyn Moriarty, "She was a true original through and through."

Another special visit was paid to our friend, Fay Bergerman during this time. Fay had been extremely devoted to her beloved husband, the late, Stanley Bergerman. After Stanley passed away Fay's health began to digress. On this visit, Fay read through a notebook that contained all of the letters she and Stanley had sent to this writer since 1995. This was our last visit with Fay Bergerman. Her kindness and her friendship will always be cherished. Fay Schiller Bergerman passed away March 4, 2005 at the age of 89.

When it came time to leave Los Angeles, in 2002, a separate smaller suitcase was purchased to pack documentation to begin research on Carla's life, which included the unfinished research that her mother Belle Laemmle began in Chicago in 1901. In addition, there were multitudes of photographs depicting Carla Laemmle's life and her family. The caches of photographs also tell her story.

The October 2003, "double birthday celebration" was different than usual. We visited Forry Ackerman at his new home on Russell Avenue. He informed us that he sold his famed "Ackermansion" on Glendower Avenue several months before, along with a vast amount of his famed science-fiction, horror and fantasy collection. Our visit was followed by dinner at The Dresden Room. And, the ever-celebrated "Uncle Forry"

Carla remembers her "Uncle Carl" on her 96th birthday and the 90th year that Mr. Laemmle opened the gate to Universal City.

sang to Carla and later accompanied us to Carla's home for birthday cake and interesting conversation.

Over the next three years, research involving the life of Carla Laemmle became steadfast. What began with weekly telephone conversations between Carla and this writer became a daily ritual.

In 2005, for her 96th birthday, Carla also celebrated the completion of the first draft of her biography given to Carla as a gift for this writer. When Carla unwrapped her gift, she said laughing:

> This is the best gift that I've been given in 96 years! Thank you! It's not every day that someone gives you the first draft of your own life story! Thank you! I shall cherish it…after I read it!

Carla Laemmle's 97th birthday marked our 10th annual "double birthday" celebration. The festivities included dinners and movies practically every day for a week, along with a house party! One morning, Carla read to this writer from the book of *The Fourth Way Teachings*, "*Psychological Commentaries on The Teaching of G.I. Gurdjieff and P.D. Ouspensky.*" By the time of departure, neither of us wanted our special time together to end.

November 22, 2006. Two American Icons: Governor Arnold Schwarzeneggar and Carla Laemmle outside of her home, soon after her 97th birthday.

Sunday, November 18, 2006, Carla was an honored guest at the 90th birthday party for Forrest J Ackerman, which was held at The Orchid Restaurant in Los Angeles. Two hundred plus persons were in attendance.

Wednesday, November 22, 2006, California Governor Arnold Schwarzenegger and his wife, Maria Shriver paid a visit to the home of Carla Laemmle. It was the Governor's first stop to deliver MEALS ON WHEELS sponsored by the St. Vincent's Hospital of Los Angeles. The couple's youngest son, Christopher, gave the meal to Carla. During the visit, each learned they had something in common. The two American cult figures began in motion pictures at Universal. Photographers shot many photographs as the 21st-century patriot met Belle Laemmle's only daughter, Carla.

As of this writing, another double-birthday celebration took place. Carla Laemmle turned 98 years of age. Her life, she feels, has been creative and productive. Carla Laemmle strives to live life with honesty, integrity, compassion and love. She has lived through 17 United States Presidents and 98 years among the rugged peaks of change thus far.

The following posthumous letter was written to Ray Cannon, by Carla Laemmle, It was dated Friday, July 20, 2007:

> Dearest One,
> My Beloved, It has been a lifetime of 30 long earth years, and the dawn of a new century, since you left me on that dark day of June 11, 1977. How could you have known my utter devastation then? My world was shattered! I only wanted to join you. I came so close.
>
> My very insides were torn apart and I all but bled to death! In the days, months and years since you left this earthly plane your comforting spirit has ever been close to me. But oh, my dearest love, how I long to embrace you and to feel the warmth of your arms around me!
>
> So greatly blessed was I to have had you in my life for 42 beautiful, creative and fulfilling years! You enriched my life in countless ways...living "the good life," awareness of the Mystery, Order and Beauty inherent to all Creation. You brought out whatever was good in me.
>
> You introduced me to the Spiritual and gentle Chinese Philosophy of Taoism, as well as that great mystical, magnetic Life Force called "Fohat."
>
> You wrote the enchanting Chinese Play, "Her Majesty the Prince" for me and transformed me into a Princess! But of all your priceless gifts to me, my Beloved, I Cherish most of all the gift of your Love!
>
> My heart overflowed with pride and joy to have shared in the creation and success of *How to Fish the*

Raymond Cannon (1892-1977) is considered the "Father of Baja California."

Pacific Coast and *The Sea of Cortez* books! How I would love to go back and relive that magical Time with you again!

But I am in another part of Time now. In exactly three months from today, I shall be celebrating my 98th year of living and learning in this training school of Life, —Planet Earth!

I know not when my journey here will come to an end, nor the Spirit that animates my body will be taking leave of it. But when that appointed time has come, my Beloved One, my freed Spirit will hasten to seek you out, be it the farthest, most distant Star in the Heavens! I Love You.
Carla.

Carla was given a Lifetime achievement award by the Southern California Motion Picture Counsel, at a Luncheon on Saturday, December 6, 2008. Actress/singer Inge Jaklin (left) is the First Vice-President of SCMPC and Tom Tangen, the producer and host are pictured here with Carla Laemmle.

Universal City, California: June 1, 2008 …

A fire that started near one of Universal City back lot soundstages was first reported at nearly 5am. An inferno eventually erupted that created two explosions. Within 12 hours, three and a half acres of the now 391 acres of the motion picture studio and theme park had been destroyed. The cause of the fire was ruled an accident from heating tools used by workers on the iconic New York Street set. This had been Universal's seventh major fire since 1930, and the third fire to hit the New York Street set since 1932. It was the first major fire at Universal since 1990. President and chief operating officer, Ron Meyer, stated in an interview that the area known as New York Street would remain vacant until it could be rebuilt. The damages were estimated to be in the millions of dollars. Carla Laemmle was interviewed by NBC soon after the fire at Universal. During the interview, Carla expressed sadness and disbelief in the wake of the disaster. She felt as if her "former home had gone up in flames." The day following the Hollywood inferno, Universal City was reopened to the public along with the studio tour. Patrons were able to see the aftermath of a truly eerie real-life fire. Carla Laemmle concluded, by saying: "It was something that you couldn't bring back. It was gone! And only the memory was left."

Epilogue

Among the many great blessings the Gods of Karma bestowed upon Carla Laemmle was her being brought in contact with the ancient esoteric Wisdom Teaching, "The Fourth Way," also known as Esoteric Christianity. Carla recalled, "It was in the late 1950s when my dear friend, Cora Galenti, loaned me her copy of "Psychological Commentaries on the Teaching of G.I. Gurdjieff and P.D. Ouspensky" by Maurice Nicoll. Its effect on me was electric. It struck an immediate chord in me. It was as if I had known this Teaching before in another life and had found it again. I learned there were five volumes in all to the Commentaries, published in London [Vincent Stuart, 1957]. I wasted no time sending for them. The Teaching has been a vital and positive force in my life, a never-ending source of great knowledge and meaning. The knowledge of this work is about reaching a higher level of being." The following are some random excerpts from the Teaching: "The Work begins with self-observation. Self-observation is a means of self-change. A man must observe everything in himself and always as if it were not himself but "It". This means he must say, "What is "It" doing?" not "what am I doing?" "These "I's" often carry on long conversations and you think it is talking to yourself. "You are thereby putting the feeling of "I" into each of the different "I's". You must withdraw the feeling of "I" from them and no longer be identified with them." "We believe we have only one "I." Is it an illusion? Our being is characterized by multiplicity, —meaning we have not one "I"—but many, many "I's" of all ages in our inner world." "We are, in a sense, where we place our consciousness. Consciousness is like light. What are we going to cast this light on?" "Where our Consciousness is, there we are. We need not place our consciousness on the negative emotions...You put yourself under the power of a person when you become negative with him or her." "We live in two worlds, outer and inner. All our happiness depends on where we are in the inner country. It is where we are inside not outside that matters." "A particular mood is a particular place in this inner country." "Moods are in opposites, the pendulum of mechanical emotions swings us from happy to depressed." "The Law of the Pendulum" is in everything. By the "Law of the Pendulum" is meant the swinging of things between opposites. Everything comes to an end and turns into its opposite in time, so that one thing is replaced by its opposite. The end of sorrow is joy, the end of weeping is

Carla concludes, "I hope to leave this stage gracefully—and with the music playing—most preferably—a Strauss Waltz," Photo of Miss Laemmle from an evening of Strauss Waltzes that she performed in the 1920s.

laughter, the end, in fact of everything we know in this life of time is its opposite. All life lies between opposites, everything we know in this life of time is its opposite." "Everything is the result of two opposite forces that tend to counterbalance one another and so to produce a balance in all things." "If we understand the Work you will see that happiness does not depend entirely on whether things go for or against you. This Work is to make something in you independent of what happens to you." "As regards attitude to life, it is much the best to think that the experience we have are necessary for us. It is the only way to get something from every experience." Carla Laemmle continues to read and re-read the Commentaries, over and over. The most important endeavor for her is to apply the teachings to the ever changing circumstances and events in life. Carla concludes, "I have no crystal ball to tell me when my allotted time here will come to an end and I must leave this earthly body. I do not fear it. I have done it before many times beyond number. I will not be sorry or sad when the Play ends. It's been a great run and learning experience, and with recurrence, there will be another embodiment and another part to play affording new opportunities for growth and the attainment of a higher level of being. So whenever the final curtain comes down and I take my final bow, I hope to leave the stage gracefully—and with the music playing—most preferably—a Strauss Waltz. " Carla Laemmle is an enchanting human being. Her hope is to continue to say yes to life at every opportunity. She continues to be blessed with good health. She has danced her way into our hearts, "among the rugged peaks," and long after the final curtain. Those who know her would agree that Carla Laemmle *is* a true love.

Notes

Act One/ CHICAGO AND THE WESTWARD MOVE/1909-1921
Scene One: Little Miss Rebekah and her Land of Dreams

1. In 1878, Michael Reese, a bachelor living in San Francisco, died on shipboard, while en route to Europe. In his will, he bequeathed to his nephews, Henry and Joseph Frank, funds to be used for charitable purposes in Chicago. They offered the money to the UHRA (United Hebrew Relief Association) for building a new hospital; while other bequests Reese left to his sister and brother-in-law were set aside as an endowment for the hospital. Additional funds were raised within the community and the hospital was opened in October 1881, at a final cost of over $70,000, that included furnishings and instruments imported from Europe. From it's beginning, Michael Reese Hospital served all people, regardless of race, religion, or national origin, and its physicians brought state- of-the-art techniques and research procedures into the field of medicine. Reese was joined as a Jewish-sponsored hospital by Maimonides Hospital in 1911 and Mount Sinai Hospital in 1919. With the sale in recent years of Michael Reese, Mount Sinai remains as the only Jewish community-supported hospital and medical center in Chicago (Online: Chicago Jewish Community).
2. The development of Washington Park on Chicago's south side began in 1869. In that year, after years of lobbying on the part of prominent south side residents, the Illinois state legislature authorized the creation of the five-member, governor-appointed South Park Commission. Members of the commission authorized a $2 million bond issue to cover the cost of acquiring over 1,500 acres of land, including that which became Washington Park. Today, Washington Park remains an important public amusement space for south side Chicagoans. The administration building is now home to the DuSable Museum of African American History (Online: Jazz Age Chicago— Washington Park).
3. Carl Laemmle was living at 378 West End Avenue in New York City then.
4. Woodrow Wilson (28th President of the United States) was a two term President between Tuesday, March 4, 1913 and Thursday, March 3, 1921. President Wilson was born Sunday, December 28, 1856 in Staunton, Virginia and died Sunday, February 3, 1924 in Washington D.C. Wilson was of the Democratic Party. Carl Laemmle was a conservative.
5. *The Birth of a Nation* was first screened in New York's Liberty Theatre, Wednesday, March 3, 1915, with an unprecedented admission price of $2.00. Public interest was so overwhelming that President Woodrow Wilson himself requested a private showing, making this the first film ever shown in the White House. The NAACP (founded in 1909) protested the picture, Saturday, December fourth of that year. The Superior Court in Fulton County, Georgia accepted the Ku Klux Klan as a new establishment. (Wilson's claim about the film was "like writing history with lightening, and my one regret is that it is all so terribly true" was reported only by Reverend Dixon's widow and has never been independently verified.) (Online: [4 pages] Organica News, Arts: Film "*The Birth of a Nation*—80 years of Controversy" by Phill Hall.)
6. Chicago's worst single disaster occurred in the summer of 1915. At 7:28 a.m. Saturday, July 24, the excursion steamer "Eastland" slowly rolled over, still moored to her dock between LaSalle and Clark Streets on the south bank of the Chicago River. Of the 2,572 persons on board, 844 perished. The passengers were Western Electric employees, their friends and family going to an annual company picnic in Michigan City, Indiana. The causes for the disaster are still subject to debate. The "Eastland" itself was rapidly refloated, towed to South Chicago, renamed the Wilmette and refitted as a naval training vessel until 1947 when she was broken up for scrap (Online: Chicago Public Library: 1915, July 24: Eastland Disaster).
7. As a matter of record, Grace Campbell's marriage to Ralph Danielson produced two children. The first, a son, James Campbell Danielson passed away four days after birth [March 21, 1917]

then a daughter, Patricia lived six years, five months and 19 days [April 19, 1928]. Grace survived her husband by nearly five years. Mr Danielson passed away at age 72, Saturday, February 6, 1965. Grace Danielson passed away at the age of 79, Thursday, October 29, 1970 (Danielson family interred at Rosehill Cemetery, Chicago, Illinois).

8. Armistice Day officially received its name in America in 1926 through Congressional resolution. It became a national holiday 12 years later by similar Congressional action. Had it not been for continuing war in Europe, Armistice Day would have been proclaimed. However, in 1954, to equally preserve the peace by veterans of WWII and make an occasion to honor those who served America in all wars, President Dwight David Eisenhower signed a bill proclaiming November 11 as Veteran's Day. (Online: First World War.com-The Armistice).

9. Known as "Spanish Flu" or "La Grippe" the influenza of 1918-1919 was a global disaster. More people died of influenza in a single year than in four years of the Black Death Bubonic Plague from 1347-1351. Of United States soldiers who died in Europe, half of them fell to the influenza virus and not to the enemy. An estimated 43,000 servicemen mobilized for WWI (also known as the "Great War") died of influenza. It infected 28% of all Americans. An estimated 675,000 Americans died as a result. (Online: The 1918 Influenza Pandemic.)

10. In two years that followed, Sunday, July 6, 1919, Thalberg was on a train from Brooklyn on route to Los Angeles with Carl Laemmle after the movie producer appointed the 20 year old his personal secretary. From that occasion, Irving Thalberg would live his life in southern California. At age 21, Thalberg was officially made general manager of Universal Pictures, a post previously occupied by Daniel Ross Lederman. Additional sources regarding Irving Thalberg were live conversations, between Carla Laemmle and the author, October 20, 1996.

11. It was arranged by family that Recha Laemmle's body be moved Wednesday, July 23, 1941 from Salem Fields Cemetery in Brooklyn, New York to the Home of Peace Mausoleum in East Los Angeles, California (Courtesy of the Home of Peace Memorial Park, Monday, October 21, 1996).

12. Saturday, June 28, 1919, the Treaty of Versailles was signed at the Hall of Mirrors and eventually ratified by Germany, France, England Italy, and Japan thus ending World War I. Although President Wilson participated in the signing of the Treaty, the United States Senate, however, voted (53-38) against the Treaty's ratification, Friday, November 19, 1920. Approval would have resulted in American participation in the League of Nations. Many as an infringement on American sovereignty opposed this participation (Online: 1919 League 2-League of Nation's Fight-A Chronology [also:] American World History: 1918-1919, World history: 1920-1921 History Central.com).

13. LCP: Chicago's Midway Airport: Review (Online: Lake Claremont Press, Aviation History Takes Off: April 24, 2003).

14. Mary Philbin and Rebekah [Carla] Laemmle would not see each other again until 1988 (some 63 years later) when the two were reunited at Mary's Fairfax Avenue home in Hollywood. The actress passed away at the age of 90, Friday, May 7, 1993 in Huntington Beach, California.

15. *Daughters of the American Revolution* (DAR) was founded October 11, 1890. It was incorporated by an Act of Congress approved, December 2, 1896. DAR currently has over 165,000 members in 3,000 chapters across the United States and internationally. Any woman 18 years or older-regardless of race, religion, or ethnic background-who can prove lineal descent from a patriot of the American Revolution, is eligible for membership (Online: DAR/National Society).

16. Maud Wood Park became the first national president of the League and thus the first League leader to rise to the challenge Online: LWV of Salinas Valley/History of the League of Women Voters of the United States [also:] (Votes for Women: Selections from the National American Women Suffrage Association Collection 1848-1921).

Act One /*Scene Two*: BETH'S UNIVERSAL EXPERIENCE/1921 – 1934

1. Peyton Randolph (1721-1775), American Patriot and Statesman, was elected President of the First Continental Congress in Philadelphia (during Monday, September 5, 1774 to Saturday, October 22, 1774, and Saturday, May 20, to Wednesday, May 24, 1775). As a member of the House of Burgesses in 1748, he was the author of protest to the King against the impending Stamp Act, but later opposed Patrick Henry's resolutions as being too radical. He was a close and personal friend to George Washington. (From the Records of Carrie Belle Laemmle.)
2. Beth kept all of her filmed birthday parties, including separate film footage of her screen test of *The Merry Widow* for Erich von Stroheim stored in her garage. After retrieving the cans of film many years later, it was discovered that they had all disintegrated (Conversations between Carla Laemmle and the author, October 18, 2003).
3. In 1926, Edward Laemmle helped to found the Temple Israel of Hollywood with seven other men. Those men were, Dr. Herman N. Appel, Isadore Bernstein, I.E. Chadwick, Jesse J. Goldburg, Joseph Miller, John Stone, and Sol Wurtzel. The Temple had several Rabbis'. Its most notable was Rabbi Max Nussbaum who began in 1942. Rabbi Nussbaum was planning his retirement in 1974 when he passed away before he could see his successor, Rabbi Haskell Bernat, be chosen. The Temple continues to thrive today. Many Jewish educational programs in wide-ranges are offered. Rabbi John L. Rosove, is the Temple's Senior Rabbi since November 1988 (Online: Temple Israel of Hollywood).
4. It all started in 1927, after a long run of Walt Disney's *Alice Comedies* at Universal. Walt decided to drop the series after signing an agreement with Universal Pictures to create a new cartoon star. Carl Laemmle suggested that the new star shouldn't be a cat, dog, or human but a rabbit. Obviously, Walt had other intentions. In 1928, *Oswald the Lucky Rabbit* was created under negotiations with the Mintz studio. Carl Laemmle handed ownership of Oswald to the young cartoonist, Walter Lantz. Young Lantz got his first big break at Universal after Laemmle selected him to make the animated opening for the full-color Universal multimillion-dollar musical, *King of Jazz* that starred Paul Whiteman. Lantz made hundreds of cartoons that brought to life such notables as Andy Panda, Chilly Willie and the incomparable Woody Woodpecker. Walter Lantz was later given an Honorary Oscar by the Academy of Motion Picture Arts and Sciences for "bringing joy and laughter to every part of the world through his unique animated motion pictures." Lantz' wife, Grace Stafford, was the voice for Woody Woodpecker from 1950 until the late 1980s. Grace Stafford passed away March 17, 1992. Walter Lantz passed away March 22, 1994. (Online: Wikipedia, the free encyclopedia.)
5. Los Angeles was incorporated as a city in the U.S. State of California, Thursday, April 4, 1850. It was initially founded September 4, 1781 as part of the Spanish controlled Mexico. The settlement was christened El Pueblo de Nuestra Senora la Reina de los angeles del Rio de Porcúincula. (Online: <u>Los Angeles</u>: Wikipedia, the free encyclopedia.)
6. The Hollywood area of Los Angeles was founded in the late 1800s. In 1903 the community was incorporated. The infamous "Hollywoodland" sign which read for many years was replaced in 1939 as "Hollywood." (Online: Limerick Leader: How Hollywood USA got its name)
7. Carl Laemmle purchased Thomas Ince's mansion, 'Dios Dorados' from his widow, Nell, in 1926 and moved in the following year. The estate was located near the Harold Lloyd estate. Laemmle's mansion was subdivided in the 1980s and Harold Lloyd's home was later razed. (Conversation with Carole Bergerman and the author, October 31, 1982)
8. Del Lord began working as a director in 1921. He was one of the original Keystone Cops. He eventually worked at Columbia Pictures directing over three dozen of producer Jules White's *The Three Stooges*. (Online: Wikipedia, the free encyclopedia)
9. Sid Grauman (1879-1950), probably the best-known exhibitor in film history broke ground for his Chinese Theatre, January 5, 1926 in the 6900 block of Hollywood Boulevard. Opening night occurred Wednesday, May 18, 1927 with the Los Angeles premiere of Cecil B. DeMille's epic production, *The King of Kings*.

10. Carl Laemmle had produced a partial-talkie version *Showboat*, in 1929 with Laura LaPlante. It hailed no great success. However, considered one of the best screen versions of *Showboat* was Universal Picture's 1936 release that starred Irene Dunne. It was produced by Carl Laemmle, Jr. along with his favorite director, James Whale. Having been credited with a cycle of horror movies at the studio for five years, *Showboat* and *Sutter's Gold* was Junior Laemmle's last attempt at a big production. *Sutter's Gold* was a bomb at the box-office. *Showboat* ultimately became Junior's swan song. MGM would later film a mediocre version of the musical in the 1950s that starred Ava Gardner. (From an interview with Carl Laemmle, Jr., and the author, July 6, 1979.)

11. A committee of seven members was given the task of creating an Academy Awards presentation. Though the idea was shelved for nearly a year due to other pressing Academy issues, the plans for an awards ceremony presented by the Awards committee were accepted in May of 1928. It was decided that all films released from August 1, 1927 through July 31, 1928 would be be eligible for the first Academy Awards.

12. The first Academy Awards ceremony was held in the Blossom Room of the Hollywood Roosevelt Hotel, May 16, 1929. Two hundred and 50 people attended the black tie banquet that evening. It was a quiet affair compared to the glamour and glitz that accompany the ceremonies of today. Though this was the first time the awards were to be given, the attendees were not anxious. Unlike the secrecy that surrounds the winners of today's ceremonies, the winners of the first Academy Award ceremony were announced three months early. The first motion picture to win an Academy Award was *Wings*.

13. George Gershwin as composer/pianist, premiered his "Rhapsody in Blue," live, Tuesday, February 12, 1924 at New York City's Aeolian Hall. Mr. Gershwin was accompanied by the Palais Royal Orchestra, conducted by Paul Whiteman. (Vienna Online: Background Sound: George Gershwin)

14. *King of Jazz* was the first all-Technicolor feature length musical film for Universal Pictures.

15. James Dietrich later worked for Walter Lantz, in television, as the Musical Director for the "Woody Woodpecker Show (1957-1972)." James Dietrich passed away in Los Angeles, California, November 7, 1984. (Courtesy of Carla Laemmle)

16. Boris Petroff was born in Sarotov, Russia, December 19, 1894. He was also a stage director on Paramount Publix stage presentations for 10 years prior to 1937. He staged *Madame DuBarry*. Petroff directed the movie *Hats Off*, released in 1936. He did not return to film work until 1949. During the 1950s, he produced a number of low budget thrillers under the name of Brooke Peters. His daughter Gloria Petroff is a type of cult figure herself. She appeared in her father's movie *The Unearthly*, released in 1957. She is seen as the "Screaming Woman". That particular brief scene appeared recently in the 2005 movie *The Upside of Anger*. Petroff was also, at one time, dramatic advisor to Mae West (1937 Motion Picture Almanac, and Carla Laemmle).

17. World Theology (volume 3)-December 1933 p.381- "Reincarnation" (vf) Carla.

18. A Brief Theosophical Definition of Devachan : (Tibetan, bde-ba-can, pronounced de-wa-chen) A translation of the Sanskrit, sukhavati, "the happy place" or god-land. It is the state between earth-lives into which the human entity withdraws itself all that aspires towards it, and takes that "all" with it into the devachan; and the atman, with the buddhi and with the higher part of the manas, become thereupon the spiritual monad of man. (Online: Devachan -A Wisdom Archive on Devachan.)

19. The Fox Carthay Theatre in Los Angeles was built in 1926. It was designed by Dwight Gibbs in the Spanish Baroque/Mission Revival style. It had 1510 seats and a grand Wurlitzer Theatre Organ. It was the site of movie premieres such as, Cecil B. DeMille's *Volga Boatman*. Walt Disney's *Snow White and the Seven Dwarfs* and David O'Selznick's *Gone With the Wind*. The theatre was torn down in 1968 because the structure was not earthquake safe. A school now occupies the sight.

20. Raymond Cannon's 1929 divorce, from Fanchon Royer, left Ray without much the way of material things. They had three children together. Fanchon also had custody of the children. Fan-

chon Royer was Hollywood's first female movie producer. She was born in Des Moines, Iowa. Fanchon Royer and Raymond Cannon married February 9, 1920. After the divorce, Fanchon eventually remarried and had two more children. In 1945, she was again divorced and moved with her five children to Puebla, Mexico, where she spent the remainder of her life. She passed away Sunday, December 13, 1981. (Courtesy of Carla Laemmle.)

21. The 12-episode serial, *Tailspin Tommy in the Great Air Mystery*, was the first serial based on a comic strip. However, it was not the first serial ever made, nor was it a big success. One of the first of "12-episode" serials that was produced by Selig Polyscope, starring a blonde actress named Kathlyn Williams. In fact, Raymond Cannon's first appearance was in *The Adventures of Kathlyn* (released in 1913). (Courtesy of Carla Laemmle)

Act Two: CARLA'S RAY OF LIGHT / Her Majesty the Prince/1935 – 1977

1. Miguel Contreras Torres was born Thursday, September 28, 1899 in Morelia, Michoacán, Mexico. Mr. Torres was a multi-talented individual in the motion picture business, both in Mexican and American film releases. He is credited as an actor, director, producer, writer, cinematographer and film editor. He made dozens of movies between 1920 and 1967. He passed away, Friday, June 5, 1981 in Mexico City, Mexico at the age of 81. (Motion Picture Almanac, 1982.)

2. In 1933, while Carla and Orion Novello were friends and rehearsing for *Romeo & Juliet*, Orion was driving Carla's automobile. They were involved in a car accident that totaled Carla's car. She hadn't seen him since then, until Helen Dietrich told her of Orion being in the play. After that evening backstage, she and Orion never saw each other again. (Carla Laemmle, 2005.)

3. Curley Robinson was a friend and confidant who was well versed in legal matters. He was acquainted with many people in Hollywood. (Courtesy of Carla Laemmle)

4. The Screen Actors' Guild really started in 1929. It started with a strike. Most Hollywood actors then belonged to Equity. Equity called a strike. It wanted better working conditions than the producers were willing to grant. Equity wasn't daring enough. It told its Hollywood members who had contracts to refuse to sign new contracts. It told members with pending contracts to refuse to sign. It told members without contracts not to go to work. The brunt of the blow fell, of course, on the little fellow, the actor without the contract. The strike collapsed in 12 weeks without having accomplished much more than keeping a few hundred actors out of work (Online: Hollywood is a Union Town Pg.1, No. 4).

5. The founders of the Screen Actors' Guild were Alan Mowbray, Ralph Morgan, Kenneth Thomson, Alden Gay, Morgan Wallace, Leon Ames, James and Lucille Gleason, Bradley Page, Claude King, Ivan Simpson, Boris Karloff, Richard Tucker, Reginald Mason, Arthur Vinton, Clay Clement, Charles Starrett, C. Aubrey Smith, Willard Robertson, Tyler Brooke, and Noel Madison. (Ibid.Pg. 2, No.7)

6. Virtually every studio in Hollywood declared bonuses that same year. This was too much even for fortuitous actors. That June, S.A.G. was incorporated. In July, virtually every actor in Hollywood was invited to a mass meeting. Only a few turned out. It got 60 members. The big shots wouldn't come in. Most of the stars were still members of the Academy. Then the NRA (National Recovery Administration) motion picture code was adopted, and the Academy promptly assumed the right to represent the actors. The NRA code was ruled unconstitutional by 1935. (Reasononline: Intolerance Alliance by Jesse Walker)

7. The Los Angeles Times (Page 8, Column 1), New Chinese Cultural Club Formed .

8. Rabbi Magnin also officiated the funeral services of Rosabelle Laemmle Bergerman and Carl Laemmle, Jr. Rabbi Edgar F. Magnin passed away Tuesday, July 17, 1984 at the age of 94.

9. Laupheim is a city in Germany in the state of Baden-Württemberg. It is situated in the region of Upper Swabia, approximately 20km north of Biberach and 20km south of Ulm on the BundesstraBe 30. The following villages now belong to Laupheim, Baustetten, Bihlafingen, Obersulmmetingen and Untersulmetingen.

10. Portions of Carla's tribute to her uncle were taken from the article "Laemmle's List," by Dr. Udo Bayer, vice-principal of the high school/junior college "The Carl Laemmle Gymnasium" in Laupheim, Württemberg, Germany, named in honor of Mr. Laemmle.
11. Earl Carroll's slogan was "THROUGH THESE PORTALS PASS THE MOST BEAUTIFUL GIRLS IN THE WORLD." Earl Carroll died in a plane crash near Mount Carmel, Pennsylvania, Thursday, June 17, 1948. Evelyn Moriarty took his accident very hard. She remembers him as a loving friend and giving person. (Conversations with Evelyn Moriarty, and the author, October 21, 1997.)
12. The late, Mr. Chow was a friend to Carla, Ray and Belle for many years. He played an integral part of the Chinese Cultural Society. He continued acting for many years and worked as a personal consultant on the *Kung-Fu* television series.
13. Excerpted from The News Gazette (Champaign, Il.) January 3, 1948, Page 3."Mrs. Campbell formerly of Urbana, Dies" (Courtesy of the Free Library, Urbana, Illinois).
14. Raymond Cannon's first published book was fully entitled, *How to Fish the Pacific Coast; a Manual for Salt Water Fisherman*. It was published in Menlo Park, California, by Lane Publishing Company, a Sunset Book 1953- 337 pages). Fish delineations by Carla Laemmle (Courtesy of Carla Laemmle).
15. In 1951, Truman raised the controversy that had been building up around American Foreign policy to a new pitch of intensity when he dismissed General Douglas MacArthur from his East Asian command for insubordination for attempting to involve the Chinese in the war and for publicly advocating an attack on China. (Infoplease: Harry S. Truman Presidency)
16. Bert Rovere (an immigrant who landed in this country at the age of 14) started the PARIS INN on East Market Street (in Los Angeles) in 1922. The Los Angeles Civic Center now stands in the original location of the PARIS INN.
17. Cannon Raymond, "The Sea of Cortez" (Menlo Park, California, A Sunset Book by Lane Publishing, 1966-283 pages). (Courtesy of Carla Laemmle)
18. Ray Cannon acknowledged Bill Burke as "William Burke" in The Sea of Cortez as one of three illustrators who contributed map drawings for the book. The other two were Michael Fahay and Peter Slaviskis. (Courtesy of Carla Laemmle)
19. Colorful Career of Ray Cannon Ends by Burt Twilegar. Western Outdoor News: Page 1 and 28 (Volume 24/No. 25/ June 17, 1977).

Act Three: MOVING FORWARD IN LIFE

1. During service to his country (in the Army Air Corps) in World War II, Lieutenant Colonel William Wyler, lost his hearing in one year as a result of the roaring of plane engines while he flew. He also supported anti-communist expression in Washington D.C. during the HUAC investigations. His mother's name was Melanie Auerbach. She was the first cousin to Carl Laemmle. She passed away, Sunday, February 13, 1955 in Hollywood of heart failure. She was 77. Wyler had a son, Billy, who passed away Sunday, November 27, 1949, at the age of three, from viral pneumonia. It all began when Carl Laemmle returned to America from Europe in 1920, the eager immigrant; Willie Wyler was first hired by Laemmle as an office boy to a casting director at Universal Pictures. He was fired for playing pool during work hours. He found temporary work at MGM, but was rehired by Universal in 1925. From 1925-1927, Willie produced some 135 *Mustang* two-reel westerns. He directed his first picture *Crook Buster* at the age of 23. William Wyler was considered the movie industry's most honored figures. He was a three time OSCAR inner. In 1965, William Wyler was honored by the Academy of Motion Picture Arts and Sciences with the Irving Thalberg Award. In 1976, William Wyler was given the Life Achievement Award for his career. The American Film Institute proudly covered some of Wyler's 41 movies. His wife, former actress, Margaret Tallichet whom he married in 1938, passed away Friday, May 3, 1991. Mr. and Mrs. Wyler had four children.

2. Incidentally, both Robert Wyler and cousin, Ernst Laemmle (a movie director in the 1920s) were born on the same day, Tuesday, September 25, 1900. Although Robert Wyler was born in Mülhausen Alsace, Germany (the same place of birth as his brother, William) and Ernst Laemmle was born in Münich Germany. Robert Wyler passed away, Sunday, January 17, 1971, in Los Angeles, California. Ernst Laemmle passed away, Monday, May 1, 1950.

3. "Why Did I Say Goodbye" words and music by Carla Laemmle was received by the Library of Congress, Friday, August 7, 1936. She worked with Mr. Lou Herscher until it was completed. Among Carla's many musical listening interests is Ragtime, preferably the music of composer Scott Joplin. She is also a fan of the "Blue Danube Waltz" and most everything else from Johann Strauss.

4. After continuing correspondence with the Regis's, Carla Laemmle and this writer later learned that Eddie Regis and his wife, Ruth Friedland Regis unfortunately passed away within weeks of each other between December 1999 and January 2000.

5. Kabbalah predates any religion or theology. The Creator gave it to mankind, without any prerequisites or preconditions. According to kabbalistic teachings, the universe operates according to certain supremely powerful principles. By learning to understand and act in accordance with these precepts, we will vastly improve our lives today, and ultimately we will achieve true fulfilment for ourselves and for all humanity. Just as basic physical laws such as gravity and magnetism exist independently of our will and awareness, the spiritual laws of the universe influence our lives every day and every moment. Kabbalah empowers us to understand and live in harmony with these laws — to use them for the benefit of us and the world. Kabbalah is much more than an intellectually compelling philosophical system. It is a precise description of the interwoven nature of spiritual and physical reality — and it is a full complement of powerful, practical methods for attaining worthy goals within that reality. Simply put, Kabbalah gives you the tools you need to achieve happiness, fulfilment, and to bring the Light of the Creator into your life. It is the way to gain peace and joy you want and deserve at the very core of your being (Online: The Kabbalah Centre-What is Kabbalah).

Selected Bibliography

Anderegg, Michael A., *William Wyler* (Twayne Publishers, USA, 1979).

Atkins, Rick, *Let's Scare 'Em!* (Grand Interviews and a Filmography of Horrific Proportions, 1930-1961) (Jefferson, North Carolina, McFarland and Company, Inc., 1997).

Bayer, Udo, *Laemmle's List*: Carl Laemmle's affidavits for Jewish Refugees [Online: 22 pages] (also published in Film History, April 1998).

Brown, Karl, *Adventures with D.W. Griffith* (New York, DaCapo Press, Inc., 1973).

Chaplin, Charles, *Charlie Chaplin: My Autobiography* (Penguin Books, 1992; reprinted from 1964 first edition).

Crowther, Bosley, *Hollywood Rajah* (New York, Dell Publishing, Inc., 1960).

Drinkwater, John, *The Life and Adventures of Carl Laemmle* (1931 reprint from a copy at the University of Illinois Library (G. P. Putnam's Sons and Arno Press, Inc. 1978).

Endres, Stacey and Cushman, Robert, *Hollywood At Your Feet, The Story of the World-Famous Chinese Theatre* (Pomegranate Press, Ltd., Los Angeles/London, 1992).

Flamini, Roland, *Thalberg: The Last Tycoon and the World of M-G-M* (New York, Crown Publishers, 1994). (Pp. 24-27.)

Gaines, Lois, *PARIS INN*; from the July 26-August 2, 1951 issue of *KEY* Dining Guide: *Food, Fun and Frolic In Southern California* Pp 22, 23, 39, and 42.

Gifford, Denis, *A Pictorial History of Horror Movies* (London, New York, Sydney and Toronto, 1973).

Griffith, Richard and Arthur Mayer, *The Movies* (New York, Simon and Schuster, 1970).

Hirschorn, Clive, *The Universal Story: The Complete History of the Studio and All Its Films* (New York, Sterling Publishing Co. Inc., Updated edition, 2001).

Kohner, Frederick, *The Magician of Sunset Boulevard*: *The Improbable Life of Paul Kohner, Hollywood Agent* (Palos Verdes, California, USA, Morgan Press, 1977).

Laemmle, Carl, *This Business of Motion Pictures*: An unpublished

1927 autobiographical, 227 page manuscript by Carl Laemmle (Excerpted for Film History, March 1983). (Pp. 47-71, Courtesy of Udo Bayer.)

Osborne, Robert, *60 Years of the Oscar: The Official History of the Academy Awards* (Abbeville Press, New York, 1989).

Pierce, David, "Carl Laemmle's Outstanding Achievement: Harry Pollard and the struggle to film Uncle Tom's Cabin" (*Film History*, Volume 10/1998) (Pp. 459-476, Courtesy of Udo Bayer.)

Schatz, Thomas, (with preface by Steven Bach), *The Genius of the System: Hollywood Filmmaking In the Studio Era* (Henry Holt and Company, 1988 and 1996).

Skal, David J., *The Monster Show: A Cultural History of Horror* (New York, Penguin Books, 1993).

Stuart, Gloria, with Sylvia Thompson, *I Just Kept Hoping* (Boston, New York, London, Little Brown and Company, 1999).

Thomas, Bob, *Walt Disney: An American Original* (New York, Hyperion—The Walt Disney Company, 1994).

_____, *Thalberg: Life and Legend* (Doubleday & Company, 1969). (Pp. 36- 47),

Variety Daily: (obituary), "Uncle Carl (Laemmle)" (Vol. 25, No. 17, front page) (September 25, 1939). (Courtesy of Carla Laemmle.)

Variety Weekly: (obituary) "Irving Grant Thalberg" (September 16, 1936). (Pp 1, 2, 62).

_____: (obituary), "Rabbi Edgar F. Magnin" (July 25, 1984).(Pg.93,94).

_____: (obituary), "William Wyler" (July 29, 1981).(Pp 2, 93).

Wray, Fay, *On the Other Hand: A Life's Story* (New York, St. Martin's Press, 1988).

Appendix

Stage and Film Credits

Stage credit as Rebekah Laemmle:

Auditorium Recital Hall-Chicago Illinois, Friday evening July 2nd, 1920 at 8:15. Three dance numbers in all by Mlle. Laemmle. She ended the evening's program with a toe dance.

Stage credit as Beth Laemmle:

1) *Sally* (Shrine Civic Auditorium, Los Angeles, February 20 to February 26, 1928).
2) *Wildflower* (Shrine Auditorium January 9 to January 16, 1928).
3) *Boccaccio* (Shrine Auditorium January 16 to January 22, 1928).
4) *Naughty Marietta* (Shrine Auditorium January 23 to January 29,1928).
5) *Prince of Pilsen* (Shrine Auditorium January 30 to February 5, 1928).
6) *No, No, Nanette* (Shrine Auditorium February 6 to February 12, 1928).
7) *The Chocolate Soldier* (Shrine Auditorium February 13 to February 19,1928).
8) *The Merry Widow* (Shrine Auditorium December 26, 1927 to January 1, 1928)

Filmography as Beth Laemmle:

1) *The Phantom of the Opera* (Universal, 1925)
2) *Don Juan* (Warner Brothers, 1926)
3) *La Boheme* (Metro-Goldwyn-Mayer, 1926)
4) *Topsy and Eva* (Universal, 1927)
5) *The Gate Crasher* (Universal, 1928)
6) *The Hollywood Revue* (MGM, 1929)
7) *The Broadway Melody* (MGM, 1929)
8) *King of Jazz* (Universal, 1930)

Filmography as (uncredited) Carla Laemmle:

9) *Waterloo Bridge* (Universal, 1931)
10) *Dracula* (Universal, 1931)
11) *Mystery of Edwin Drood* (Universal, 1935)
12) *The Adventures of Frank Merriwell* (Universal, 1936, 12-episode serial)

Filmography as Carol Lenard (uncredited in the following):

13) *The Great Waltz* (Metro-Goldwyn-Mayer, 1938)
14) *On Your Toes* (Warner Brothers, 1939)
15) *The Chocolate Soldier* (Metro-Goldwyn-Mayer, 1941)
16) *Mission to Moscow* (Warner Brothers, 1943)
17) *Step Lively* (RKO, 1944)
18) *George White's Scandals* (RKO, 1945)
19) *Night and Day* (Warner Brothers, 1946)

Miscellaneous (Carla Laemmle)

20) *The Vampire Hunter's Club* (Irene Belle Films, 2001: Carla was credited as "elder Vampire." Forry Ackerman and actress Mink Stole also appeared in this movie.)

Special appearances as herself (Carla Laemmle):

1) *Universal Horror* (1998 for television) (Carla appears in clips and interviews.)
2) Hosted *The Road to Dracula*, 1999 Documentary DVD release that accompanied both the English and Spanish versions of "Dracula," Universal Pictures, 1931.
3) *Opera Ghost: A Phantom Unmasked* (Universal Home Video, 2000).
4) *The Phantom of the Opera: The Ultimate Edition* ("Carla Laemmle Remembers," a Video Interview with David Skal.) (Milestone Collection, 2003).

Carla Laemmle Photo Archive

Carla's maternal grandmother, Emma Norton on her 85th birthday

Carrie "Belle" Norton, 1889 college freshman portrait

The distinguished Joseph Laemmle (c. 1895)

Carla Laemmle (front right) with the ladies of China City welcoming the public to the Ancient Autumn Moon Ritual (Los Angeles, August 2, 1941).

Carla's paternal grandmother, Rebekkah Laemmle (1831-1883)

Carla's paternal grandfather Julius Baruch Laemmle (1820-1892)

Reunion after 64 years: Mary Philbin and Carla Laemmle, at Mary's home, on Fairfax Avenue in Hollywood(1988)

Joseph Laemmle at home, Universal City, California (1927)

Carla clowning with "Trixie the Laughing Show Horse" (1929)

The widower Carl Laemmle, with his daughter, Rosabelle Laemmle, age fourteen, and son Julius, age six, at Universal City, California, 1915.
Below Left: Carla winter 1917; Below Right: Carla dressed for Halloween 1916

Among the Rugged Peaks

Index

Abbott, George 64, 104
Academy Awards 197, 202
Academy of Motion Picture Arts and Sciences, The 58, 196, 199
Ackerman, Forrest J 9, 166-168, 170, 187
Actor's Equity 104
Adventures of Frank Merriwell, The 79, 96, 204
Adventures of Kathlyn, The 198
Alexander, Max 46
Alice Comedies 196
Allgar, Bridget 132
All Quiet on the Western Front 63, 64, 71, 111, 150
American Guild of Variety Artists (AGVA) 104
Anything Goes (play) 47, 80, 81
Arbuckle, Fatty 48
Auditorium Recital Hall (Chicago, Illinois) 203
Ayres, Lew 64
Baja California 117, 121, 128, 130, 133, 145, 189
Balanchine, George 104, 113
Balatka, Dr. 26
Barondess, Barbara 87
Battle Creek Sanitarium, The 18
Bayer, Dr. Udo 12, 169, 170 172, 174, 175, 181, 184, 199, 202
Belcher, Ernest 10, 40, 44, 45, 55
Belcher, Marge Celeste 44
Bergerman, Carol 100. 133, 141, 149, 154, 158, 164
Bergerman, Stanley 11, 52, 63 72, 82, 83, 95, 105, 107, 110, 139, 164, 169, 171, 172, 184, 185
Bernheim, Julius 50, 52, 53, 152, 153
Bernstein, Isadore 24, 152, 196
Beidermann, Paula (first Mrs. Joseph Laemmle) 16
Birth of a Nation, The 25, 194

B'hai Faith, The 14
Blind Husbands 49
Boccaccio (operetta-play) 58, 203
Bohéme, La 55, 203
Bride of Frankenstein, The 81
Briggs, Donald 79
Broadway Melody, The 59, 61, 62, 64, 203
Burke, Bill (William) 133-139, 199
Campbell, Mrs. Carrie (Loomis) 25, 27, 30, 55
Campbell, James A. 28, 121
Canaan, Connecticut 30
Cannon, Raymond (Ray) 13, 14, 78, 80, 83, 85, 100-102, 114, 117, 120, 121, 124, 128, 130, 133, 136, 141, 142, 160, 166, 181, 184, 188, 189, 197, 199
Carroll, Earl 115, 199
Champion, Marge and Gower 44
Chaney, Lon 10, 26, 51, 54, 55, 64, 68, 69
Chaplin, Charlie 47, 48, 50, 57, 201
Chicago, Illinois 10, 19, 20, 25, 27, 195
China City (Los Angeles) 14, 83, 84, 101, 122
Chinese Culture Society 14, 101, 102, 114, 120, 130
Chocolate Soldier, The (operetta-play) 58, 203
Chocolate Soldier, The (movie) 111, 204
Chow, David 102, 117
Civil War, The 14
Cleveland, Grover 13
Colebrook River, Connecticut 14
Columbia Pictures 64, 196
Continental Clothing Company 17
Coolidge, Calvin 66
Cowdin, J. Cheever 84
Crosby, Bing 66
Danielson, Mrs. Grace (Campbell) 25, 27, 28, 30, 55, 121, 130, 194 195
Danielson, James Campbell 28, 194

Danielson, Patricia Grace 195
Danielson, Ralph 25, 27, 30, 194
DAR (*Daughters of the American Revolution*) 30, 41, 43, 59, 72, 121, 132, 195
Davis, Donald 123-127
Dietrich, Helen 67, 68, 85, 198
Dietrich, James (or Jimmy) 66-68, 141, 158, 197
Disney, Walt 47, 59, 196, 197, 202
Dios Dorados (home of Carl Laemmle) 152, 196
Don Juan (1926) 55, 203
Dracula (1931-movie) 2, 10, 46, 68-71, 111, 166, 170, 179, 182, 204
Drinkwater, John 201
Duffy, Henry 80
Edison Patents Company 21
Eisenhower, Dwight David 195
Fairbanks, Douglas 50, 57
Family Theatre, The (Muscatine, Iowa) 17
Fellows, Edith 115
Fields, Willon 55, 56, 86-88
Fillmore, Millard 13
First National Pictures (see also: Warner Brothers) 47, 78, 88
Fleckles Anna (Stern) 23, 29, 107
Fleckles, Maurice 23, 152
Foolish Wives 49, 64
Ford, Gerald R. 13
Fourth Way, The (book) 186, 191
Fox Carthay Theatre, The (Carthay Circle Theatre, Los Angeles) 197
Galenti, Cora 119, 126, 191
Gamble, Baxter 96
Gate Crasher, The 59, 60, 203
Gayne, Homer 74-78
George White's Scandals (1945) 115, 116, 204
Gershwin, George 66, 67, 197
Goldwyn Pictures 56
Grant, Ulysses, S. 13
Great United States Depression 66
Grauman, Sid (Grauman's Chinese Theatre, Los Angeles) 57, 196

Griffith, D.W. 44, 143, 201
Hiawatha (1909) 22
Hall, (Rev.) Manly P. (Palmer) 102, 141
Heller, Frieda 22, 155
Heller, Peppi 47, 155
Her Majesty the Prince (play of 1936) 13, 80, 84, 85, 160, 161, 163, 188, 198
Hitler, Adolf (or Hitler) 83, 100, 177
Hollywood Bowl, The 44, 86
Hollywood Land (sign) 196
Hollywood Roosevelt Hotel 197
Holm, Eleanor 150
Hoover, Herbert C. 66
Houdini (the camel) 39
"How to Fish the Pacific Coast" (book) 121, 124, 126, 128, 199
HUAC (House of Un-American Activities Committee) 100, 199
Hunchback of Notre Dame, The (1923) 64
Illinois Staatszeitung (publication) 16, 17
Ichenhausen, Germany 22, 47
Ince, Thomas 48, 196
Independent Motion Picture Company (IMP) 21-24
Influenza Epidemic (1918-1919) 28, 29, 195
Jacobson, Professor Henri 25, 26
Jazz Singer, The 57
Julian, Rupert 52
Kanakoff, Ruthe 141, 145-149
Kennedy, John F. 132
King of Jazz 65-67, 196, 197, 203
Kira, Gene 166
Kohner, Frederick 201
Kohner, Paul 44, 46, 152, 201
Korean War 122, 123, 125-127
LaPlante, Laura 46, 81, 197
Laemmle, Belle
(also: Carrie "Belle" Norton Laemmle or Belle Norton)
(a.k.a. Mrs. Joseph Laemmle) 10, 13-15, 18, 19, 30, 41-43, 63, 72, 84, 99, 101, 102, 132,

119, 121, 130, 132, 185, 188, 196
Laemmle, Carla 10-18, 19-33, 34-79, 80-144, 145-190, 191-193, 195-198, 200, 202, 204
(a.k.a. Beth Laemmle) 10, 34, 55, 57, 58, 60, 66, 67, 203
(a.k.a. Rebekah Laemmle and Rebekah Isabelle Laemmle) 10, 19, 20, 27, 34, 35, 38, 203
(a.k.a. Carol Lenard) 34, 104, 116, 128, 204
Laemmle, Carl 10, 11, 16, 17, 22-24, 29, 30-32, 34, 45, 47, 49-52, 54, 56, 57, 59, 63, 65,
   72, 80, 82, 83, 98-100, 104, 105, 107-111, 127, 133, 139, 155, 166, 169, 171-173,
   174-177, 179-181, 184, 194-197, 199, 201, 202
Laemmle, (Julius) Carl, Jr., 22, 29, 56, 63, 65, 70, 71, 82, 83, 97, 111, 152, 197, 198
Laemmle, (Bernheim) Karoline 15, 16, 177
Laemmle, Edward 17, 45, 46, 72, 151, 155, 181, 196
Laemmle, Eleanor 153-155, 158
Laemmle. Ernst 45, 56, 152, 199, 200
Laemmle Film Service 21, 23
Laemmle, Joseph 14, 15, 17-19, 21, 22, 30-32, 35, 41, 44, 49, 52, 53, 56, 58, 63, 84
Laemmle, Julius (Baruch)
(a.k.a. J.B. Laemmle) 15, 16, 176, 177
Laemmle, Louis 15-17, 19, 22, 23, 29, 47, 56, 107, 127, 153-155, 177
Laemmle, Nina 152
Laemmle, Rebekkah (Mrs. Julius Baruch) 15, 16, 176, 177
Laemmle, Richard 153-158
Laemmle, Rosabelle
(a.k.a. Rosabelle Laemmle Bergerman) 22, 29, 30, 51, 52, 56, 72, 98, 104, 107, 110,
   130-132, 139, 140, 155, 171, 198

Laemmle, Siegfried 15, 16, 56, 99, 107, 127, 152, 173, 177
Langdon, Harry 39, 50
Lantz, Walter 196, 197
Laupheim, Germany (Baden Wurttemberg) 9, 12, 15, 16, 34, 99, 100, 106, 108, 111,
   169-185, 198
Lawrence, Florence 21
Leroux, Gaston 51
Loomis, Amelia (Long) (Mrs. Oliver Porter Loomis) 14, 30
Loomis, Joseph 132
Loomis, Oliver Porter 14
Lord, Del 57, 196
Los Angeles, California 14, 18, 32, 43, 44, 57-59, 71, 72, 74, 85, 97, 100, 101, 106, 116,
   122, 130, 132, 136, 141, 146, 154, 155, 163, 166, 168, 169, 172, 180, 183, 185, 187,
   195-200
Los Angeles Natural History Museum 85
Lugosi, Bela 11, 69, 168, 182
Luke, Keye 102
Lusitania, The 25
MacRae, Henry 78, 79
MacLean, Douglas (Mrs.) 87
Magnificent Obsession 82, 83
Magnin, Rabbi Edgar F. 98, 106, 198, 202
Malchow, Raliegh J. 40, 41
Manners, David 78
Masonic Temple (Chicago, Illinois) 14
Matray, Ernst & Maria 113, 114, 116
Mayer, Louis B. 51, 56
Merry Widow, The (operetta-play) 58, 203
Merry Widow, The (movie) 196
Metro-Goldwyn-Mayer 56, 64, 203, 204
Michael Reese Hospital (Chicago, Illinois) 19
Mickey Mouse 59
Mission to Moscow 111, 204
Monroe, Marilyn 115, 185
Moriarty, Evelyn 114, 115, 149, 169,

184, 185, 199
Music Box Theatre (Los Angeles) 84,
"My Land of Dreams" (poem by Carla Laemmle) 32, 33, 54
Mystery of Edwin Drood 78, 204
Nardini, Dr, Talatt 53
NBC (National Broadcasting Company) 34, 173, 190
Naughty Marietta (operetta-play) 58, 203
Nussbaum, Rabbi 196
Newberry Library of Chicago, The 13
Nicoll, Maurice 191
Night and Day 116, 117, 204
No No Nanette (operetta-play) 58, 203
Norton, Edward Daniel 14, 30
Norton, Emogene Isabella Loomis (a.k.a. Emma Norton) 10, 14, 18, 21, 23, 25, 29, 30, 32, 39, 43, 84, 98, 121, 132
Novello, Orion 74, 75, 92, 93, 198
Olmstead, Gertrude 30
On Your Toes (play) 104,
On Your Toes (1939-movie) 103.104.204
Opera Ghost: A Phantom Unmasked 204
Oshkosh, Wisconsin 17, 22
Oswald the Lucky Rabbit 196
Ouspensky, P.D. 186, 191
Paramount Pictures 49, 64, 73, 197
Paris Inn 122-125, 199, 201
Park, Maud Wood 195
Perry, Barbara 78, 115
Peter the Hermit 37
Petroff, Boris 71, 73, 197
Phantom of the Opera, The (1925 movie) 10, 26, 51, 52, 54, 55, 71, 203, 204
Philbin, Mary 26, 27, 30, 31, 44, 54, 55, 195
Philbin, Mrs. Blanche (mother of Mary Philbin) 26, 30, 44
Philbin, Mr. John (father of Mary Philbin) 26, 30, 44
Pickford, Mary 22, 44, 57,
Porter, Cole 117

Prince of Pilsen (operetta-play) 58, 203
Princess Quan Mui Mai 13, 84, 163,
Prohibition (in America) 28, 47
Radio Corporation of America (RCA) 29
Randolph, Peyton 41, 43, 132, 196
Reagan, Ronald (Wilson) 114
Remarque, Erich Maria 63
Rin Tin Tin 50
Road to Dracula, The (DVD documentary) 182, 183, 204
Rogers, Charles (movie executive) 84
Rogers, Jean 79
Rosehill Cemetery (Chicago, Illinois) 195
Royer, Fanchon 197, 198
Rhythm Boys, The 66
Sally (operetta play) 58, 203
Samurai (1945) 117
Screen Actor's Guild, The 99, 198
Sea of Cortez (at the Baja peninsula) 117, 118, 130, 140, 142, 142, 144, 145
"Sea of Cortez, The" (book) 133, 137, 140, 141, 151, 189, 199
Showboat (movie versions) 44, 81, 83, 197
Showboat (play) 57
Shrine Civic Auditorium (Los Angeles, California) 56, 58, 59, 71, 203
Sommers, Lawrence 85, 102, 158-164
Stafford, Grace 196
Stahl, John 83,
Standard Capital Corporation 82, 83, 172
Stern, Recha (Rachel) (a.k.a. Mrs. Carl Laemmle) 17, 22, 23, 29, 173, 195
Stern, Sam 22
Step Lively 111-114, 204
Sutter's Gold 82, 90, 197
Tailspin Tommy in the Great Air Mystery 78, 198
Taft, William Howard 19, 28
Taylor, Ray 79
Taylor, William Desmond 48
Temple, Shirley 44, 100
Temple Israel of Hollywood 196

Thalberg, Henrietta 29
Thalberg, Irving (Grant) 29, 30-32, 45, 50-52, 56, 59, 62, 95, 97, 98, 106, 110, 153, 195, 199, 201
Thalberg, Sylvia 45
Three Stooges, The 196
Titanic (ship) 22
Torres, Miguel 85, 88, 198
Topsy and Eva (1927) 57, 203
Traffic in Souls 49
Trixie ("the Laughing Show Horse") 39-41, 45
Unforgettable Sea of Cortez, The (book) 166, 179, 181
United Artists Company 57
University of Illinois (Urbana/Champaign), The 14, 25, 42, 201
Universal City 10, 11, 23, 24, 28, 29, 30-32, 34-41, 44-46, 49-53, 55-59, 60, 63-69, 71,
  75, 78-84 98, 107, 109-111, 150-154, 166, 168, 169, 172, 173, 182-184, 186, 188,
  190, 195-197, 199, 201, 203, 204,
Universal Horror (1998-TV) 204
Universal Film Manufacturing Company 24, 29
Universal Pictures 10, 11, 24, 30, 34, 41, 53, 57, 59, 80, 82, 173, 184, 195-197, 199
Urbana, Illinois 14, 15, 19, 121, 199
Valentino, Rudolf 50
Vampire Hunter's Club, The 183, 204
Von Stroheim, Erich 49, 52, 53, 196
Warner Brothers
(also: First National Pictures)
(Warner Bros.) 56, 57, 64, 78, 103, 104, 111, 116, 117, 203, 204
Waterloo Bridge 204
West, Mae 37, 197
Whale, James 18, 83, 197
White, George 114
White, Mary (of the Joseph Loomis family) 132
White, Jules 196

White Front Theatre, The 17, 21
Whiteman, Paul 65, 196, 197
Wildflower (operetta-play) 58, 203
Williams, Clark 79
Wilson, Mrs. Florence (publicist for Universal Pictures, 1925) 53, 54
Wilson, Woodrow 24, 27, 29, 194
Wings (1927 movie) 197
World War I, 195
World War II, 155, 163, 199
Women's Suffrage 195
World Theology ("Reincarnation" by Carla Laemmle) 72-74, 197
Woody Woodpecker 196, 197
Xochimilco (Mexico) 96, 140,
Zehner, Harry 32
Zorina, Vera 104

If you enjoyed this book
please call or write
or e-mail
for a free catalog.

Midnight Marquee Press, Inc.
9721 Britinay Lane
Baltimore, MD 21234

410-665-1198

www.midmar.com